CIVIL RIGHTS DECISIONS OF THE UNITED STATES SUPREME COURT THE 19th CENTURY

MAUREEN HARRISON & STEVE GILBERT
EDITORS

CIVIL RIGHTS DECISIONS SERIES

EXCELLENT BOOKS
SAN DIEGO, CALIFORNIA

R-cy

EXCELLENT BOOKS
Post Office Box 927105
San Diego, CA 92192-7105

Publisher's Cataloging in Publication Data

Civil Rights Decisions Of The United States Supreme Court: The 19th Century/
  Maureen Harrison, Steve Gilbert, editors.
  p. cm. - (Civil Rights Decisions Series)
Bibliography: p.
Includes Index.
1. Civil Rights - United States - Cases, 2. United States. Supreme Court.
I. Title. II. Harrison, Maureen. III. Gilbert, Steve.
IV. Series: Civil Rights Decisions.
KF4748 H24 1994   LC 93-74635
342.'73-dc20
ISBN 1-880780-04-6

INTRODUCTION

Who can speak the blessedness of that first day of freedom? Is not the sense of liberty a higher and finer one than any of the five? To move, speak, and breathe, go out and come in unwatched, and free from danger! Who can speak the blessings of that rest which comes down on the free man's pillow, under laws which insure to him the rights that God has given to man.

Harriet Beecher Stowe
Uncle Tom's Cabin

The Constitution's promise of civil rights, "the blessings of liberty to ourselves and our posterity," or what Harriet Beecher Stowe called the "laws which insure to free men the rights that God has given to them," did not, throughout most of the the nineteenth century, apply to America's non-white minorities: Native, African, and Chinese Americans. Federal, state, and municipal laws treated these racial minorities as trespassers, as property, and as invaders. Seeking protection from oppressive and unjust laws, individual Native, African, and Chinese Americans appealed, on their own behalf and on behalf of all their fellows, to the United States Supreme Court to enforce the Constitution's promise of civil rights. In this book you will find their pleas and the Court's replies.

Civil Rights Decisions: The 19th Century, the first of two volumes, places into the hands of the reader what we consider to be the Supreme Court's most important civil rights decisions for the years 1831 through 1896, the post-Revolutionary War period through the American Civil War, into the Reconstruction Era, and up to the turn of the Century. This book is divided into three sections: **The Native Americans, The African Americans** and **The Chinese Americans**. In each we have selected for their legal and historic significance the Court's civil rights decisions that best represent nineteenth century America's treatment of these three racial minorities.

THE NATIVE AMERICAN CASES

The only good Indian is a dead Indian. - **Philip Sheridan**

The only true Americans found their peace treaties with the "Great White Father" to be worthless. In this book you will find three nineteenth century decisions on Native American civil rights: **The Trail of Tears Cases,** two decisions which chronicle the legal fight to halt the exile of the Cherokees Nation from their homeland, and **The Native American Citizenship Case**, which denies citizenship to "Indians, born within the United States."

THE AFRICAN AMERICAN CASES

The soul of one man cannot by human law be made the property of another. - **John Quincy Adams**

The pre-Civil War Supreme Court wrestled several times with the issue of slavery and the post-Civil War Court with the legalization of segregation. In this book you will find six nineteenth century decisions on African American civil rights: **The Fugitive Slave Cases**, two challenges to the constitutionality of the Fugitive Slave Acts, **The Great Slavery Case**, *The Dred Scott Decision*, which could only be overturned by a civil war, and **The Segregation Cases**, which legally segregated America for sixty years.

THE CHINESE AMERICAN CASES

Give me your tired, your poor. - **Emma Lazarus**

The Constitution gives Congress to power to regulate, for good or ill, immigration and naturalization. In this book you will find two nineteenth century decisions on Chinese American civil rights: **The Chinese Exclusion Case**, which banned Chinese immigration, deported Chinese residents, and denied American citizenship to those remaining, and **The Chinese Laundry Law Case**, San Francisco's attempt to drive "Chinatown" out of business.

The United States Supreme Court is the Court of Last Appeal in all cases concerning Constitutional rights and protections. The Justices of the Court, appointed by the President and approved by the Congress, have decided many famous and and equally infamous constitutional cases dealing with the civil rights of Native, African, and Asian Americans. The selected Civil Rights Decisions presented in this book are carefully edited versions of the official texts issued by the Supreme Court in *United States Reports.* Judge Learned Hand wrote: "The language of the law must not be foreign to the ears of those who are to obey it." We, as editors, have made every effort to make the the language of these decisions less "foreign." We have attempted to replace esoteric legalese with plain English without damaging the original decisions. Edited out are long alpha-numeric legal citation and wordy wrangles over abstract points of procedure. Edited in are definitions (writ of habeas corpus = an order from a judge to bring a person to court), translations (certiorari = the decision of the Court to review a case), identifications (Appellant = Dred Scott, Appellee = John Sandford), and explanations (who the parties were, who the members of the Court were, what laws were at issue, what constitutional provisions were involved, where the case originated, how the case reached the court, and what the final decision was).

You will find in this book the opinion of the Court as expressed by the Justice chosen to speak for the majority. Preceding each edited decision we provide a brief history of the case, we note where the complete unedited decision can be found, and we give the members of the Court deciding the case. The bibliography provides a selected list of further reading on the cases and the Court. Also included for the reader's reference is a complete copy of the United States Constitution, to which every decision refers.

On July 4, 1854 Henry David Thoreau addressed an Independence Day Rally in Framingham, Massachusetts. Thoreau said then of the Supreme Court's Civil Rights decisions: "The Judges . . . try [these cases] by a very low and incompetent standard. They consider, not whether the [law] is right, but whether it is what they call *constitutional*"; Supreme Court Justice John Marshall Harlan, who followed Thoreau's ideal to consider whether the law was right, was the lone dissenter in 1896's *Plessy v. Ferguson* Separate But Equal Decision. Nearly sixty years ahead of his time he wrote: Our Constitution is color-blind, and neither knows nor tolerates classes among its citizens. In respect of civil rights, all citizens are equal before the law. . . . The law regards a man as a man, and takes no account . . . of his color when his civil rights as guaranteed by the supreme law of the law are involved."

Supreme Court Justice Oliver Wendell Holmes, Jr. wrote in *The Common Law*: "In order to know what the law is, we must know what it has been." We hope that **Civil Rights Decisions,** published in the fortieth anniversary year of *Brown v. Board of Education,* and only two years shy of the hundreth anniversary of *Plessy v. Ferguson,* will let you know, in Justice Holmes' phrase, "what the law has been," and will give you an understanding of the prevailing attitudes towards the civil rights of racial minorities in the nineteenth century and how those attitudes carried over into and colored the decisions to come in the twentieth.

We begin this book with the words of the man to whom it is dedicated, Dr. Martin Luther King, Jr., who said of civil rights: "I have a dream that one day this nation will rise up, live out the true meaning of its creed: We hold these truths to be self-evident, that all men are created equal."

M.H. & S.G.

This book is dedicated to the memory of
The Reverend Dr. Martin Luther King, Jr.
1929 - 1968

It may be true that morality cannot be
legislated, but behavior can be regulated.
It may be true that the law cannot make a
man love me, but it can keep him from
lynching me, and I think that's pretty
important.

Life is breathed into a judicial decision by
the persistent exercise of legal rights until
they become usual and ordinary in human
experience.

One has not only a legal but a moral
responsibility to obey just laws.
Conversely, one has a moral responsibility
to disobey unjust laws.

I have a dream
that one day this nation will rise up,
live out the true meaning of its creed:
We hold these truths to be self-evident, that
all men are created
equal.

TABLE OF CONTENTS

THE NATIVE AMERICAN CASES

If it be true that the Cherokee Nation have rights, this is not the tribunal in which those rights are to be asserted. If it be true that wrongs have been inflicted, and still greater are to be apprehended, this is not the tribunal which can redress the past or prevent the future.

Chief Justice John Marshall (1831)

The Cherokees acknowledge themselves to be under the protection of the United States. . . . Protection does not imply the destruction of the protected.

Chief Justice John Marshall (1832)

The plaintiff [John Elk, an Indian, born within the United States], not being a citizen of the United States under the Fourteenth Amendment to the constitution, has been deprived of no right secured by the Fifteenth Amendment, and cannot maintain this action.

Justice Horace Grey (1884)

THE AFRICAN AMERICAN CASES

THE FUGITIVE SLAVE CASES

Prigg v. Pennsylvania
59

[W]e have not the slightest hesitation in holding, that under and in virtue of the constitution, the owner of a slave is clothed with the entire authority, in every state in the Union, to seize and recapture his slave. . . .

Justice Joseph Story (1842)

Ableman v. Booth
85

[I]n the judgment of this court, the act of Congress commonly called the Fugitive slave law is, in all its provisions, fully authorized by the Constitution. . . .

Chief Justice Roger Taney (1859)

THE GREAT SLAVERY CASE

Dred Scott v. Sandford
93

[T]hat unfortunate race . . . had for more than a century before been regarded as beings of an inferior order, and altogether unfit to associate with the white race . . . so far inferior, that they had no rights which the white man was bound to respect.

Chief Justice Roger Taney (1857)

THE SEGREGATION CASES

The Slaughterhouse Cases
115

Was it the purpose of the Fourteenth Amendment, by the simple declaration that no State should make or enforce any law which shall abridge the privileges and immunities of citizens of the United States, to transfer the security and protection of all civil rights which we have mentioned, from the States to the Federal government?

Justice Samuel Miller (1873)

The Civil Rights Cases
139

When a man has emerged from slavery, and by the aid of beneficent legislation has shaken off the inseparable concomitants of that state, there must be some stages in the progress of his elevation when he takes the rank of a mere citizen, and ceases to be the special favorite of the laws, and when his rights as a citizen, or a man, are to be protected.

Justice Joseph Bradley (1883)

THE SEPARATE BUT EQUAL CASE

Plessy v. Ferguson
163

If the civil and political rights of both races be equal, one cannot be inferior to the other civilly or politically. If one race be inferior to the other socially, the Constitution of the United States cannot put them upon the same plane.

Justice Henry Brown (1896)

THE CHINESE AMERICAN CASES

The Chinese Laundry Case

Yick Wo v. Hopkins

179

Though, the law itself be fair on its face and impartial in appearance, yet, if it is applied and administered by a public authority with an evil eye and an unequal hand, so as practically to make unjust and illegal discrimination between persons in similar circumstances, material to their rights, the denial of equal justice is still within the prohibition of the Constitution.

Justice Stanley Matthews (1886)

The Chinese Exclusion Case

Chae Chan Ping v. United States

187

If, therefore, the government of the United States, through its legislative department, considers the presence of foreigners of a different race in this country, who will not assimilate with us, to be dangerous to its peace and security, their exclusion is not to be stayed. . . .

Justice Stephen Field (1889)

THE NATIVE AMERICAN CASES

The Cherokee Nation v. Georgia

From time immemorial the Cherokee Nation have composed a sovereign and independent State, and in this character have been repeatedly recognized by the United States, in various treaties subsisting between their nation and the United States.

John Ross, Chief of the Cherokee Nation
December 27, 1830

From time immemorial a part of the Cherokee Nation lived between the Savannah and Altamaha rivers in what is now Georgia. The Cherokee Nation sought protection from white settlers by signing treaties (the Hopewell Treaty in 1785 and the Holston Treaty in 1791) with the United States in which the Cherokee Nation was recognized as a sovereign and independent state under the protection of the United States. The Cherokees were guaranteed by these, and other treaties, and by an Act of Congress dated March 30, 1802, the right to self-government without interference from any State or the United States.

In the late 1820's gold was discovered on Cherokee lands. On December 12, 1829 Georgia passed a law entitled "An Act to add the Territory of the Cherokee Indians to Carroll, DeKalb, Gwinett, Hall and Habersham Counties." The law seized all Cherokee lands; abolished all Cherokee laws, and ended the Cherokee Nation's political existence. The Georgia militia was to enforce the law.

When President Andrew Jackson refused to honor the U.S. Government's treaty obligation to protect the Cherokee Nation, they petitioned the United States Supreme Court to protect them from the State of Georgia.

On March 18, 1831 Chief Justice John Marshall announced the 5-2 decision of the Court. The edited text follows.

THE CHEROKEE NATION COURT

Chief Justice John Marshall
Appointed by President John Adams
Served 1801 - 1835

Associate Justice William Johnson
Appointed by President Jefferson
Served 1804 - 1834

Associate Justice Joseph Story
Appointed by President Madison
Served 1811 - 1845

Associate Justice Gabriel Duvall
Appointed by President Madison
Served 1811 - 1835

Associate Justice Smith Thompson
Appointed by President Monroe
Served 1823 - 1843

Associate Justice John McLean
Appointed by President Van Buren
Served 1829 - 1861

Associate Justice Henry Baldwin
Appointed by President Jackson
Served 1830 - 1844

The unedited text of *The Cherokees v. Georgia* can be found on page 1, volume 30 of *United States Reports.*

THE CHEROKEE NATION v. GEORGIA
March 18, 1831

CHIEF JUSTICE MARSHALL: This bill is brought by the Cherokee Nation, praying an injunction [court order to stop an action] to restrain the State of Georgia from the execution of certain laws of that State, which, as is alleged, go directly to annihilate the Cherokees as a political society, and to seize, for the use of Georgia, the lands of the nation which have been assured to them by the United States in solemn treaties repeatedly made and still in force.

If courts were permitted to indulge their sympathies, a case better calculated to excite them can scarcely be imagined. A people once numerous, powerful, and truly independent, found by our ancestors in the quiet and uncontrolled possession of an ample domain, gradually sinking beneath our superior policy, our arts and our arms, have yielded their lands by successive treaties, each of which contains a solemn guarantee of the residue, until they retain no more of their formerly extensive territory than is deemed necessary to their comfortable subsistence. To preserve this remnant the present application is made.

Before we can look into the merits of the case, a preliminary inquiry presents itself. Has this court jurisdiction of the cause?

The third article of the Constitution describes the extent of the judicial power. The second section closes an enumeration of the cases to which it is extended, with "controversies" "between a State or the citizens thereof, and foreign states, citizens, or subjects." A subsequent clause of the same section gives the Supreme Court original jurisdiction in all cases in which a State shall be a party. The party defendant [Georgia] may then unquestionably be sued in this court. May the plaintiff [Cherokee Nation] sue in it? Is the Cherokee Nation a foreign state in the sense in which that term is used in the Constitution?

The counsel for the [Cherokee Nation] have maintained the affirmative of this proposition with great earnestness and ability. So much of the argument as was intended to prove the character of the Cherokees as a State, as a distinct political society separated from others, capable of managing its own affairs and governing itself, has, in the opinion of a majority of the judges, been completely successful. They have been uniformly treated as a State from the settlement of our country. The numerous treaties made with them by the United States recognize them as a people capable of maintaining the relations of peace and war, of being responsible in their political character for any violation of their engagements, or for any aggression committed on the citizens of the United States by any individual of their community. Laws have been enacted in the spirit of these treaties. The acts of our government plainly recognize the Cherokee Nation as a State, and the courts are bound by those acts.

A question of much more difficulty remains. Do the Cherokees constitute a foreign state in the sense of the Constitution?

The counsel have shown conclusively that they are not a State of the Union, and have insisted that individually they are aliens, not owing allegiance to the United States.

An aggregate of aliens composing a State must, they say, be a foreign state. Each individual being foreign, the whole must be foreign.

This argument is imposing, but we must examine it more closely before we yield to it. The condition of the Indians in relation to the United States is perhaps unlike that of any other two people in existence. In the general, nations not owing a common allegiance are foreign to each other. The term *foreign nation* is, with strict propriety, applicable by either to the other. But the relation of the Indians to the United States is marked by peculiar and cardinal distinctions which exist nowhere else.

The Indian Territory is admitted to compose a part of the United States. In all our maps, geographical treaties, histories and laws, it is so considered. In all our intercourse with foreign nations, in our commercial regulations, in any attempt at intercourse between Indians and foreign nations, they are considered as within the jurisdictional limits of the United States, subject to many of those restraints which are imposed upon our own citizens. They acknowledge themselves in their treaties to be under the protection of the United States; they admit that the United States shall have the sole and exclusive right of regulating the trade with them, and managing all their affairs as they think proper; and the Cherokees in particular were allowed by the treaty of Hopewell, which preceded the Constitution, "to send a deputy of their choice, whenever they think fit, to Congress." Treaties were made with some tribes by the State of New York under a then unsettled construction of the confederation, by which they ceded all their lands to that State, taking back a limited grant to themselves, in which they admit their dependence.

Though the Indians are acknowledged to have an unquestionable, and, heretofore, unquestioned right to the lands they occupy until that right shall be extinguished by a voluntary cession to our government, yet it may well be doubted whether those tribes which reside within the acknowledged boundaries of the United States can, with strict accuracy, be denominated foreign nations. They may, more correctly, perhaps, be denominated domestic dependent nations. They occupy a territory to which we assert a title independent of their will, which must take effect in point of possession when their right of possession ceases. Meanwhile they are in a state of pupilage. Their relation to the United States resembles that of a ward to his guardian.

They look to our government for protection; rely upon its kindness and its power; appeal to it for relief to their wants; and address the President as their great father. They and their country are considered by foreign nations, as well as by ourselves, as being so completely under the sovereignty and dominion of the United States, that any attempt to acquire their lands, or to form a political connection with them, would be considered by all as an invasion of our territory, and an act of hostility.

These considerations go far to support the opinion that the framers of our Constitution had not the Indian tribes in view when they opened the courts of the Union to controversies between a State or the citizens thereof, and foreign states.

In considering this subject, the habits and usages of the Indians in their intercourse with their white neighbors ought not to be entirely disregarded. At the time the Constitution was framed, the idea of appealing to an Ameri-

can court of justice for an assertion of right or a redress
of wrong, had perhaps never entered the mind of an Indian or of his tribe. Their appeal was to the tomahawk,
[not] to the government. This was well understood by the
statesmen who framed the Constitution of the United
States, and might furnish some reason for omitting to enumerate them among the parties who might sue in the
courts of the Union. Be this as it may, the peculiar relations between the United States and the Indians occupying
our territory are such that we should feel much difficulty
in considering them as designated by the term *foreign
State*, were there no other part of the Constitution which
might shed light on the meaning of these words. But we
think that in construing [interpreting] them, considerable
aid is furnished by that clause in the eighth section of the
third article, which empowers Congress to "regulate commerce with foreign nations, and among the several States,
and with the Indian tribes."

In this clause they are as clearly contradistinguished by a
name appropriate to themselves from foreign nations as
from the several States composing the Union. They are
designated by a distinct appellation; and as this appellation can be applied to neither of the others, neither can
the appellation distinguishing either of the others be in
fair construction applied to them. The objects to which
the power of regulating commerce might be directed, are
divided into three distinct classes - foreign nations, the
several States, and Indian tribes. When forming this article, the convention considered them as entirely distinct.
We cannot assume that the distinction was lost in framing
a subsequent article, unless there be something in its language to authorize the assumption.

The counsel for the plaintiffs [Cherokee Nation] contend that the words "Indian tribes" were introduced into the article empowering Congress to regulate commerce for the purpose of removing those doubts in which the management of Indian affairs was involved by the language of the ninth article of the confederation. Intending to give the whole power of managing those affairs to the government about to be instituted, the convention conferred it explicitly; and omitted those qualifications which embarrassed the exercise of it as granted in the confederation. This may be admitted without weakening the construction which has been intimated. Had the Indian tribes been foreign nations, in the view of the convention, this exclusive power of regulating intercourse with them might have been, and most probably would have been, specifically given in language indicating that idea, not in language contradistinguishing them from foreign nations. Congress might have been empowered "to regulate commerce with foreign nations, including the Indian tribes, and among the several States." This language would have suggested itself to statesmen who considered the Indian tribes as foreign nations, and were yet desirous of mentioning them particularly.

It has been also said that the same words have not necessarily the same meaning attached to them when found in different parts of the same instrument: their meaning is controlled by the context. This is undoubtedly true. In common language the same word has various meanings, and the peculiar sense in which it is used in any sentence is to be determined by the context. This may not be equally true with respect to proper names. Foreign nations is a general term, the application of which to Indian tribes, when used in the American Constitution, is at best extremely questionable. In one article in which a power is

given to be exercised in regard to foreign nations generally, and to the Indian tribes particularly, they are mentioned as separate in terms clearly contradistinguishing
them from each other. We perceive plainly that the Constitution in this article does not comprehend Indian tribes
in the general term "foreign nations;" not, we presume, because a tribe may not be a nation, but because it is not
foreign to the United States. When, afterwards, the term
"foreign State" is introduced, we cannot impute to the
convention the intention to desert its former meaning, and
to comprehend Indian tribes within it, unless the context
force that construction on us. We find nothing in the
context, and nothing in the subject of the article, which
leads to it.

The court has bestowed its best attention on this question,
and, after mature deliberation, the majority is of opinion
that an Indian tribe or nation within the United States is
not a foreign state in the sense of the Constitution, and
cannot maintain an action in the courts of the United
States.

A serious additional objection exists to the jurisdiction of
the court. Is the matter of the bill the proper subject for
judicial inquiry and decision? It seeks to restrain a State
from the forcible exercise of legislative power over a
neighboring people asserting their independence, their
right to which the State denies. On several of the matters
alleged in the bill, for example on the laws making it
criminal to exercise the usual powers of self-government
in their own country by the Cherokee Nation, this court
cannot interpose, at least in the form in which those matters are presented.

That part of the bill which respects the land occupied by the Indians and prays the aid of the court to protect their possession, may be more doubtful. The mere question of right might perhaps be decided by this court in a proper case with proper parties. But the court is asked to do more than decide on the title. The bill requires us to control the Legislature of Georgia, and to restrain the exertion of its physical force. The propriety of such an interposition by the court may be well questioned. It savors too much of the exercise of political power to be within the proper province of the judicial department. But the opinion on the point respecting parties makes it unnecessary to decide this question.

If it be true that the Cherokee Nation have rights, this is not the tribunal in which those rights are to be asserted. If it be true that wrongs have been inflicted, and that still greater are to be apprehended, this is not the tribunal which can redress the past or prevent the future.

The motion for an injunction is denied.

In Cherokee Nation v. Georgia, *the United States Supreme Court refused, on a technicality of their own creation, to rule on the legality of the Georgia Acts and the validity of the Cherokee Treaties. The following year, American missionary Samuel Worcester brought the legal plight of the Cherokee Nation back to the Court for a final determination.*

THE NATIVE AMERICAN CASES

Worcester v. Georgia

All white persons residing within the limits of the Chero-kee Nation on the 1st day of March next, or anytime thereafter, without permission of the Governor shall be guilty of a high misdemeanor and shall be punished by confinement in the penitentiary at hard labor.

An Act of Georgia, December 22, 1830

On December 22, 1830 Georgia passed a law entitled, "An Act to prevent white persons from residing within that part of Georgia occupied by the Cherokee Indians."

Samuel Worcester, a missionary, residing within the Cherokee Nation, with the permission of the Cherokees, but without the permission of the Governor of Georgia, was arrested in July 1831 for violating the December 22nd Act. He was tried in the Gwinnett County Superior Court, found guilty, and sentenced to four years hard labor. Worcester appealed to the Supreme Court. He asserted that Georgia had no jurisdiction within the Cherokee Nation and that their Acts of December 12, 1829, in which they claimed jurisdiction, and December 22, 1830, on which he had been convicted, were in violation of the treaties still in force between the United States and the Cherokee Nation. Worcester brought back before the Supreme Court the issues they had refused to rule on the previous year in *The Cherokee Nation v. Georgia.* The Supreme Court's refusal had been based on the grounds that the Cherokees were a "domestic dependent nation" with no right to file suit in a U.S. Court. Samuel Worcester, a citizen of Vermont, had no such restriction.

On March 2, 1832 Chief Justice John Marshall announced the 6-1 decision of the Court. The edited text follows.

THE WORCESTER COURT

Chief Justice John Marshall
Appointed by President John Adams
Served 1801 - 1835

Associate Justice William Johnson
Appointed by President Jefferson
Served 1804 - 1834

Associate Justice Joseph Story
Appointed by President Madison
Served 1811 - 1845

Associate Justice Gabriel Duvall
Appointed by President Madison
Served 1811 - 1835

Associate Justice Smith Thompson
Appointed by President Monroe
Served 1823 - 1843

Associate Justice John McLean
Appointed by President Van Buren
Served 1829 - 1861

Associate Justice Henry Baldwin
Appointed by President Jackson
Served 1830 - 1844

The unedited text of *Worcester v. Georgia* can be found on page 515, volume 31 of *United States Reports*.

WORCESTER v. GEORGIA
March 2, 1832

CHIEF JUSTICE MARSHALL: This cause, in every point of view in which it can be placed, is of the deepest interest.

The defendant [Georgia] is a State, a member of the Union, which has exercised the powers of government over a people who deny its jurisdiction, and are under the protection of the United States.

The plaintiff [Worcester] is a citizen of the State of Vermont, condemned to hard labor for four years in the penitentiary of Georgia, under color of an act which he alleges to be repugnant to the Constitution, laws, and treaties of the United States.

The legislative power of a State, the controlling power of the Constitution and laws of the United States, the rights, if they have any, the political existence of a once numerous and powerful people, the personal liberty of a citizen, are all involved in the subject now to be considered.

. . . . The indictment charges the plaintiff [Worcester] and others, being white persons, with the offense of "residing within the limits of the Cherokee Nation without a license," and "without having taken the oath to support and defend the constitution and laws of the State of Georgia."

[Worcester] filed the following plea [in the state court]:

"And the said Samuel A. Worcester, in his own proper person, comes and says that this court

ought not to take further cognizance of the action and prosecution aforesaid, because, he says,
that on the 15th day of July, in the year 1831, he
was, and still is, a resident in the Cherokee Nation; and that the said supposed crime or crimes,
and each of them, were committed, if committed
at all, at the town of New Echota, in the said
Cherokee Nation, out of the jurisdiction of this
court, and not in the County Gwinnett, or elsewhere, within the jurisdiction of this court; and
this defendant saith that he is a citizen of the
State of Vermont, one of the United States of
America, and that he entered the aforesaid Cherokee Nation in the capacity of a duly authorized
missionary of the American Board of Commissioners for Foreign Missions, under the authority
of the President of the United States, and has not
since been required by him to leave it; that he
was, at the time of his arrest, engaged in preach-
ing the Gospel to the Cherokee Indians, and in
translating the sacred Scriptures into their language, with the permission and approval of the
said Cherokee Nation, and in accordance with the
humane policy of the government of the United
States for the civilization and improvement of
the Indians; and that his residence there, for this
purpose, is the residence charged in the aforesaid
indictment; and this defendant further saith that
this prosecution the State of Georgia ought not to
have or maintain, because, he saith, that several
treaties have, from time to time, been entered
into between the United States and the Cherokee
Nation of Indians [between November 1785 and
February 1819], all which treaties have been duly
ratified by the Senate of the United States of

America, and by which treaties the United States of America acknowledge the said Cherokee Nation to be a sovereign nation, authorized to govern themselves, and all persons who have settled within their territory, free from any right of legislative interference by the several States composing the United States of America, in reference to acts done within their own territory; and by which treaties the whole of the territory now occupied by the Cherokee Nation on the east of the Mississippi has been solemnly guaranteed to them; all of which treaties are existing treaties at this day, and in full force.

"By these treaties . . . the aforesaid territory is acknowledged to lie without the jurisdiction of the several States composing the Union of the United States; and it is thereby specially stipulated that the citizens of the United States shall not enter the aforesaid territory, even on a visit, without a passport from the governor of a State, or from some one duly authorized thereto by the President of the United States; all of which will more fully and at large appear by reference to the aforesaid treaties. And this defendant saith, that the several acts charged in the bill of indictment were done, or omitted to be done, if at all, within the said territory so recognized as belonging to the said nation, and so, as aforesaid, held by them, under the guarantee of the United States; that, for those acts, the defendant is not amenable to the laws of Georgia, nor to the jurisdiction of the courts of the said State: and that the laws of the State of Georgia, which profess to add the said territory to the several adjacent counties of the

said State, and to extend the laws of Georgia over
the said territory and persons inhabiting the
same; and, in particular, the act on which this indictment against this defendant is grounded, to
wit, 'An Act entitled an Act to prevent the exercise of assumed and arbitrary power by all persons under pretext of authority from the Cherokee Indians, and their laws, and to prevent white
persons from residing within that part of the
chartered limits of Georgia occupied by the
Cherokee Indians, and to provide a guard for the
protection of the gold mines, and to enforce the
laws of the State within the aforesaid territory,'
are repugnant to the aforesaid treaties; which, according to the Constitution of the United States,
compose a part of the supreme law of the land;
and that these laws of Georgia are, therefore, unconstitutional, void, and of no effect; that the
said laws of Georgia are also unconstitutional and
void, because they impair the obligation of the
various contracts formed by and between the
aforesaid Cherokee Nation and the said United
States of America, as above recited; also, that the
said laws of Georgia are unconstitutional and
void, because they interfere with, and attempt to
regulate and control the intercourse with the said
Cherokee Nation, which, by the said Constitution,
belongs exclusively to the Congress of the United
States; and because the said laws are repugnant to
the statute of the United States, passed [in]
March, 1802, entitled 'An Act to regulate trade
and intercourse with the Indian tribes, and to preserve peace on the frontier;' and that, therefore,
this court has no jurisdiction to cause this defendant to make further or other answer to the said

bill of indictment, or further to try and punish
this defendant for the said supposed offense or
offenses alleged in the bill of indictment, or any
of them; and, therefore, this defendant prays
[asks] judgment whether he shall be held bound
to answer further to said indictment."

This plea was overruled by the court, and the prisoner, being arraigned [charged with an offense], pleaded not
guilty. The jury found a verdict against him, and the
court sentenced him to hard labor in the penitentiary for
the term of four years.

.... It is, ... we think, too clear for controversy, that the
act of Congress by which this court is constituted, has giv-
en it the power, and of course imposed on it the duty, of
exercising jurisdiction in this case. This duty, however
unpleasant, cannot be avoided. Those who fill the judicial
department have no discretion in selecting the subjects to
be brought before them. We must examine the defense
set up in this plea. We must inquire and decide whether
the act of the Legislature of Georgia under which
[Worcester] has been prosecuted and condemned, be consistent with, or repugnant to the Constitution, laws and
treaties of the United States.

.... [T]he particular statute and section on which the indictment is founded ... enacts that "all white persons, residing within the limits of the Cherokee Nation on the 1st
day of March next, or at any time thereafter, without a license or permit from his excellency the governor, or from
such agent as his excellency the governor shall authorize
to grant such permit or license, and who shall not have
taken the oath hereinafter required, shall be guilty of a
high misdemeanor, and, upon conviction thereof, shall be

punished by confinement to the penitentiary, at hard labor for a term not less than four years."

The eleventh section authorizes the governor, should he
deem it necessary for the protection of the mines, or the
enforcement of the laws in force within the Cherokee Nation, to raise and organize a guard, etc.

The thirteenth section enacts, "that the said guard or any
member of them, shall be, and they are hereby authorized
and empowered to arrest any person legally charged with
or detected in a violation of the laws of this State, and to
convey, as soon as practicable, the person so arrested, before a justice of the peace, judge of the superior, or justice of inferior court of this State, to be dealt with according to law."

The extraterritorial power of every Legislature being limited in its action to its own citizens or subjects, the very
passage of this act is an assertion of jurisdiction over the
Cherokee Nation. . . .

The first step, then, in the inquiry which the Constitution
and laws impose on this court, is an examination of the
rightfulness of this claim.

America, separated from Europe by a wide ocean, was in-
habited by a distinct people, divided into separate nations,
independent of each other and of the rest of the world,
having institutions of their own, and governing themselves
by their own laws. It is difficult to comprehend the
proposition that the inhabitants of either quarter of the
globe could have rightful original claims of dominion
over the inhabitants of the other, or over the lands they
occupied; or that the discovery of either by the other

should give the discoverer rights in the country discovered which annulled the pre-existing rights of its ancient possessors.

After lying concealed for a series of ages, the enterprise of Europe, guided by nautical science, conducted some of her adventurous sons into this western world. They found it in possession of a people who had made small progress in agriculture or manufactures, and whose general employment was war, hunting, and fishing.

Did these adventurers, by sailing along the coast and occasionally landing on it, acquire for the several governments to whom they belonged, or by whom they were commissioned, a rightful property in the soil from the Atlantic to the Pacific; or rightful dominion over the numerous people who occupied it? Or has nature, or the great Creator of all things, conferred these rights over hunters and fishermen, on agriculturists and manufacturers?

But power, war, conquest, give rights, which, after possession, are conceded by the world; and which can never be controverted by those on whom they descend. We proceed, then, to the actual state of things, having glanced at their origin, because holding it in our recollection might shed some light on existing pretensions.

The great maritime powers of Europe discovered and visited different parts of this continent at nearly the same time. The object was too immense for any one of them to grasp the whole, and the claimants were too powerful to submit to the exclusive or unreasonable pretensions of any single potentate. To avoid bloody conflicts, which might terminate disastrously to all, it was necessary for the nations of Europe to establish some principle which all would acknowledge, and which should decide their respective rights as between themselves. This principle, suggested by the actual state of things, was, "That discovery gave title to the government by whose subjects or by whose authority it was made, against all other European governments, which title might be consummated by possession."

This principle, acknowledged by all Europeans, because it was the interest of all to acknowledge it, gave to the nation making the discovery, as its inevitable consequence, the sole right of acquiring the soil and of making settlements on it. It was an exclusive principle which shut out the right of competition among those who had agreed to it; not one which could annul the previous rights of those who had not agreed to it. It regulated the right given by discovery among the European discoverers, but could not affect the rights of those already in possession, either as aboriginal occupants, or as occupants by virtue of a discovery made before the memory of man. It gave the exclusive right to purchase, but did not found that right on a denial of the right of the possessor to sell.

The relation between the Europeans and the natives was determined in each case by the particular government which asserted and could maintain this pre-emptive privilege in the particular place. The United States succeeded to all the claims of Great Britain, both territorial and political; but no attempt, so far as is known, has been made to enlarge them. So far as they existed merely in theory, or were in their nature only exclusive of the claims of other European nations, they still retain their original character, and remain dormant. So far as they have been practically exerted, they exist in fact, are understood by both parties, are asserted by the one, and admitted by the other.

Soon after Great Britain determined on planting colonies in America, the king granted charters to companies of his subjects, who associated for the purpose of carrying the views of the crown into effect, and of enriching themselves. The first of these charters was made before possession was taken of any part of the country. They purport, generally, to convey the soil, from the Atlantic to the South Sea. This soil was occupied by numerous and warlike nations, equally willing and able to defend their possessions. The extravagant and absurd idea that the feeble settlements made on the sea-coast, or the companies under whom they were made, acquired legitimate power by them to govern the people, or occupy the lands from sea to sea, did not enter the mind of any man. They were well understood to convey the title which, according to the common law of European sovereigns respecting America, they might rightfully convey, and no more. This was the exclusive right of purchasing such lands as the natives were willing to sell. The crown could not be understood to grant what the crown did not affect to claim, nor was it so understood.

The power of making war is conferred by these charters on the colonies, but defensive war alone seems to have been contemplated. In the first charter to the first and second colonies, they are empowered, "for their several defenses, to encounter, expulse, repel, and resist, all persons who shall, without license," attempt to inhabit "within the said precincts and limits of the said several colonies, or that shall enterprise or attempt at any time hereafter the least detriment or annoyance of the said several colonies or plantations."

. . . . These motives for planting the new colony are incompatible with the lofty ideas of granting the soil and all its inhabitants from sea to sea. They demonstrate the truth that these grants asserted a title against Europeans only, and were considered as blank paper so far as the rights of the natives were concerned. The power of war is given only for defense, not for conquest.

The charters contain passages showing one of their objects to be the civilization of the Indians and their conversion to Christianity - objects to be accomplished by conciliatory conduct and good example; not by extermination.

. . . . Certain it is, that our history furnishes no example, from the first settlement of our country, of any attempt on the part of the crown to interfere with the internal affairs of the Indians, farther than to keep out the agents of foreign powers, who, as traders or otherwise, might seduce them into foreign alliances. The king purchased their lands when they were willing to sell, at a price they were willing to take; but never coerced a surrender of them. He also purchased their alliance and dependence by subsidies; but never intruded into the interior of their affairs, or interfered with their self-government, so far as respected themselves only.

. . . . Such was the policy of Great Britain towards the Indian nations inhabiting the territory from which she excluded all other Europeans; such her claims, and such her practical exposition of the charters she had granted: she considered them as nations capable of maintaining the relations of peace and war; of governing themselves, under her protection; and she made treaties with them, the obligation of which she acknowledged.

This was the settled state of things when the war of our Revolution commenced. The influence of our enemy was established; her resources enabled her to keep up that influence, and the colonists had much cause for the apprehension that the Indian nations would, as the allies of Great Britain, add their arms to hers. This, as was to be expected, became an object of great solicitude to Congress. Far from advancing a claim to their lands, or asserting any right of dominion over them, Congress resolved "that the securing and preserving the friendship of the Indian nations appears to be a subject of the utmost moment to these colonies."

The early journals of Congress exhibit the most anxious desire to conciliate the Indian nations. Three Indian departments were established, and commissioners appointed in each, "to treat with the Indians in their respective departments, in the name and on the behalf of the United Colonies, in order to preserve peace and friendship with the said Indians, and to prevent their taking any part in the present commotions."

The most strenuous exertions were made to procure those supplies on which Indian friendships were supposed to depend; and everything which might excite hostility was avoided.

The first treaty was made with the Delawares, in September, 1778.

The language of equality in which it is drawn evinces the temper with which the negotiation was undertaken, and the opinion which then prevailed in the United States.

. . . . During the war of the Revolution, the Cherokees took part with the British. After its termination, the United States, though desirous of peace, did not feel its necessity so strongly as while the war continued. Their political situation being changed, they might very well think it advisable to assume a higher tone, and to impress on the Cherokees the same respect for Congress which was before felt for the King of Great Britain. This may account for the language of the Treaty of Hopewell. There is the more reason for supposing that the Cherokee chiefs were not very critical judges of the language, from the fact that every one makes his mark; no chief was capable of signing his name. It is probable the treaty was interpreted to them.

The treaty is introduced with the declaration that "the commissioners plenipotentiary of the United States give peace to all the Cherokees, and receive them into the favor and protection of the United States of America. . . ."

The general law of European sovereigns, respecting their claims in America, limited the intercourse of Indians, in a great degree, to the particular potentate whose ultimate right of domain was acknowledged by the others. This was the general state of things in time of peace. It was sometimes changed in war. The consequence was that their supplies were derived chiefly from that nation, and their trade confined to it. Goods, indispensable to their comfort, in the shape of presents, were received from the same hand. What was of still more importance, the strong hand of government was interposed to restrain the disorderly and licentious from intrusions into their country, from encroachments on their lands, and from those acts of violence which were often attended by reciprocal murder. The Indians perceived in this protection only what was beneficial to themselves - an engagement to punish aggressions on them. It involved, practically, no claim to their lands, no dominion over their persons. It merely bound the nation to the British crown as a dependent ally, claiming the protection of a powerful friend and neighbor, and receiving the advantages of that protection, without involving a surrender of their national character.

This is the true meaning of the stipulation, and is undoubtedly the sense in which it was made. Neither the British government nor the Cherokees ever understood it otherwise.

The same stipulation entered into with the United States, is undoubtedly to be [interpreted] in the same manner. They receive the Cherokee Nation into their favor and protection. The Cherokees acknowledge themselves to be under the protection of the United States, and of no other power. Protection does not imply the destruction of the protected. . . .

The treaty of Hopewell seems not to have established a solid peace. To accommodate the differences still existing between the State of Georgia and the Cherokee Nation, the Treaty of Holston was negotiated in July, 1791. The existing Constitution of the United States had been then adopted, and the government, having more intrinsic capacity to enforce its just claims, was perhaps less mindful of high sounding expressions denoting superiority. We hear no more of giving peace to the Cherokees. The mutual desire of establishing permanent peace and friendship, and of removing all causes of war, is honestly avowed, and, in pursuance of this desire, the first article declares that there shall be perpetual peace and friendship between all the citizens of the United States of America and all the individuals composing the Cherokee Nation.

The second article repeats the important acknowledgment that the Cherokee Nation is under the protection of the United States of America, and of no other sovereign whosoever.

. . . . The Indian nations were, from their situation, necessarily dependent on some foreign potentate for the supply of their essential wants, and for their protection from lawless and injurious intrusions into their country. That power was naturally termed their protector. They had been arranged under the protection of Great Britain; but the extinguishment of the British power in their neighborhood, and the establishment of that of the United States in its place, led naturally to the declaration, on the part of the Cherokees, that they were under the protection of the United States, and of no other power. They assumed the relation with the United States which had before subsisted with Great Britain.

This relation was that of a nation claiming and receiving the protection of one more powerful, not that of individuals abandoning their national character, and submitting as subjects to the laws of a master.

. . . . From the commencement of our government Congress has passed acts to regulate trade and intercourse with the Indians; which treat them as nations, respect their rights, and manifest a firm purpose to afford that protection which treaties stipulate. All these acts, and especially that of 1802, which is still in force, manifestly consider the several Indian nations as distinct political communities, having territorial boundaries, within which their authority is exclusive, and having a right to all the lands within those boundaries, which is not only acknowledged, but guaranteed by the United States.

In 1819, Congress passed an Act for promoting those humane designs of civilizing the neighboring Indians, which had long been cherished by the executive. It enacts, "that, for the purpose of providing against the further decline and final extinction of the Indian tribes adjoining to the frontier settlements of the United States, and for introducing among them the habits and arts of civilization, the President of the United States shall be, and he is hereby authorized, in every case where he shall judge improvement in the habits and condition of such Indians practicable, and that the means of instruction can be introduced with their own consent, to employ capable persons, of good moral character, to instruct them in the mode of agriculture suited to their situation; and for teaching their children in reading, writing and arithmetic; and for performing such other duties as may be enjoined, according to such instructions and rules as the President may give and prescribe for the regulation of their conduct in the discharge of their duties."

This act avowedly contemplates the preservation of the Indian nations as an object sought by the United States, and proposes to effect this object by civilizing and converting them from hunters into agriculturists. Though the Cherokees had already made considerable progress in this improvement, it cannot be doubted that the general words of the act comprehend them. Their advance in the "habits and arts of civilization," rather encouraged perseverance in the laudable exertions still farther to meliorate their condition. This act furnishes strong additional evidence

of a settled purpose to fix the Indians in their country by
giving them security at home.

The treaties and laws of the United States contemplate the
Indian territory as completely separated from that of the
States; and provide that all intercourse with them shall be
carried on exclusively by the government of the Union. Is
this the rightful exercise of power, or is it usurpation?

While these States were colonies, this power, in its utmost
extent, was admitted to reside in the crown. When our
revolutionary struggle commenced, Congress was composed of an assemblage of deputies acting under specific
powers granted by the legislatures, or conventions of the
several colonies. It was a great popular movement, not
perfectly organized; nor were the respective powers of
those who were intrusted with the management of affairs
accurately defined. The necessities of our situation produced a general conviction that those measures which concerned all, must be transacted by a body in which the representatives of all were assembled, and which could command the confidence of all: Congress, therefore, was considered as invested with all the powers of war and peace,
and Congress dissolved our connection with the mother
country, and declared these United Colonies to be independent States. Without any written definition of powers,
they employed diplomatic agents to represent the United
States at the several courts of Europe; offered to negotiate treaties with them, and did actually negotiate treaties
with France. From the same necessity, and on the same
principles, Congress assumed the management of Indian
affairs; first in the name of these United Colonies, and afterwards in the name of the United States. Early attempts
were made at negotiation, and to regulate trade with them.
These not proving successful, war was carried on under

the direction, and with the forces of the United States, and the efforts to make peace by treaty were earnest and incessant. The confederation found Congress in the exercise of the same powers of peace and war, in our relations with Indian nations, as with those of Europe.

Such was the state of things when the confederation was adopted. That instrument surrendered the powers of peace and war to Congress and prohibited them to the States, respectively, unless a State be actually invaded, "or shall have received certain advice of a resolution being formed by some nation of Indians to invade such State, and the danger is so imminent as not to admit of delay till the United States in Congress assembled can be consulted." This instrument also gave the United States in Congress assembled the sole and exclusive right of "regulating the trade and managing all the affairs with the Indians, not members of any of the States: provided that the legislative power of any State within its own limits be not infringed or violated."

The ambiguous phrases which follow the grant of power to the United States were so construed by the States of North Carolina and Georgia as to annul the power itself. The discontents and confusion resulting from these conflicting claims produced representations to Congress, which were referred to a committee, who made their report in 1787. The report does not assent to the construction of the two States, but recommends an accommodation, by liberal cessions of territory, or by an admission on their part of the powers claimed by Congress. The correct exposition of this article is rendered unnecessary by the adoption of our existing Constitution. That instrument confers on Congress the powers of war and peace; of making treaties, and of regulating commerce with foreign nations, and among the several States, and with the Indian tribes. These powers comprehend all that is required for the regulation of our intercourse with the Indians. They are not limited by any restrictions on their free actions. The shackles imposed on this power, in the confederation, are discarded.

The Indian nations had always been considered as distinct, independent political communities, retaining their original natural rights, as the undisputed possessors of the soil from time immemorial, with the single exception of that imposed by irresistible power, which excluded them from intercourse with any other European potentate than the first discoverer of the coast of the particular region claimed: and this was a restriction which those European potentates imposed on themselves, as well as on the Indians. The very term "nation," so generally applied to them, means "a people distinct from others." The Constitution, by declaring treaties already made, as well as those to be made, to be the supreme law of the land, has adopted and sanctioned the previous treaties with the Indian nations, and consequently admits their rank among those powers who are capable of making treaties. The words "treaty" and "nation" are words of our own language, selected in our diplomatic and legislative proceedings, by ourselves, having each a definite and well understood meaning. We have applied them to Indians, as we have applied them to the other nations of the earth. They are applied to all in the same sense.

Georgia herself has furnished conclusive evidence that her former opinions on this subject concurred with those entertained by her sister States, and by the government of the United States. Various acts of her Legislature have been cited in the argument, including the contract of ces-

sion made in the year 1802, all tending to prove her acquiescence in the universal conviction that the Indian nations possessed a full right to the lands they occupied, until that right should be extinguished by the United States,
with their consent; that their territory was separated from
that of any State within whose chartered limits they might
reside, by a boundary line, established by treaties; that,
within their boundary, they possessed rights with which
no State could interfere, and that the whole power of regulating the intercourse with them was vested in the United States. . . . Her new series of laws, manifesting her
abandonment of these opinions, appears to have commenced in December, 1828.

In opposition to this original right, possessed by the undisputed occupants of every country; to this recognition of
that right, which is evidenced by our history, in every
change through which we have passed, is placed the charters granted by the monarch of a distant and distinct region, parceling out a territory in possession of others
whom he could not remove and did not attempt to remove, and the cession made of his claims by the Treaty of
Peace.

The actual state of things at the time, and all history since,
explain these charters; and the King of Great Britain, at
the Treaty of Peace, could cede only what belonged to his
crown. These newly asserted titles can derive no aid from
the articles so often repeated in Indian treaties; extending
to them, first, the protection of Great Britain, and afterwards that of the United States. These articles are associated with others, recognizing their title to self-
government. The very fact of repeated treaties with them
recognizes it; and the settled doctrine of the law of nations is that a weaker power does not surrender its inde-

pendence - its right to self-government, by associating with a stronger and taking its protection. A weak State in order to provide for its safety, may place itself under the protection of one more powerful without stripping itself of the right of government, and ceasing to be a State. Examples of this kind are not wanting in Europe. "Tributary and feudatory states," says Vattel, "do not thereby cease to be sovereign and independent states so long as self-government and sovereign and independent authority are left in the administration of the state." At the present day, more than one State may be considered as holding its right of self-government under the guaranty and protection of one or more allies.

The Cherokee Nation, then, is a distinct community, occupying its own territory, with boundaries accurately described, in which the laws of Georgia can have no force, and which, the citizens of Georgia have no right to enter but with the assent of the Cherokees themselves or in conformity with treaties and with the acts of Congress. The whole intercourse between the United States and this nation is, by our Constitution and laws, vested in the government of the United States.

The act of the State of Georgia under which [Worcester] was prosecuted is consequently [null and] void. . . . Can this court revise and reverse it?

If the objection to the system of legislation lately adopted by the Legislature of Georgia in relation to the Cherokee Nation was confined to its extraterritorial operation, the objection, though complete, so far as respected mere right, would give this court no power over the subject. But it goes much further. If the review which has been taken be correct, and we think it is, the acts of Georgia are repug-

nant to the Constitution, laws, and treaties of the United
States.

They interfere forcibly with the relations established between the United States and the Cherokee Nation, the regulation of which, according to the settled principles of our
Constitution, are committed exclusively to the government
of the Union.

They are in direct hostility with treaties, repeated in a
succession of years, which mark out the boundary that
separates the Cherokee country from Georgia; guaranty to
them all the land within their boundary; solemnly pledge
the faith of the United States to restrain their citizens
from trespassing on it; and recognize the pre-existing
power of the nation to govern itself.

They are in equal hostility with the acts of Congress for
regulating this intercourse, and giving effect to the
treaties.

The forcible seizure and abduction of [Worcester], who
was residing in the nation with its permission, and by authority of the President of the United States, is also a violation of the acts which authorize the chief magistrate to
exercise this authority.

Will these powerful considerations avail [Worcester]? We
think they will. He was seized and forcibly carried away
while under guardianship of treaties guarantying the
country in which he resided, and taking it under the protection of the United States. He was seized while performing under the sanction of the chief magistrate of the
Union those duties which the humane policy adopted by
Congress had recommended. He was apprehended, tried,

and condemned, under color of a law which has been shown to be repugnant to the Constitution, laws, and treaties of the United States. Had a judgment, liable to the same objections, been rendered for property, none would question the jurisdiction of this court. It cannot be less clear when the judgment affects personal liberty, and inflicts disgraceful punishment, if punishment could disgrace when inflicted on innocence. [Worcester] is not less interested in the operation of this unconstitutional law than if it affected his property. He is not less entitled to the protection of the Constitution, laws, and treaties of his country.

. . . . It is the opinion of this court that the judgment of the Superior Court for the County of Gwinnett, in the State of Georgia, condemning Samuel A. Worcester to hard labor in the penitentiary of the State of Georgia for four years, was pronounced by that court under color of a law which is void, as being repugnant to the Constitution, treaties, and laws of the United States, and ought, therefore, to be reversed and annulled.

President Andrew Jackson possessed a near pathological hatred of Native Americans, whom he called "savages" and "barbarians" and "butchers." Legend holds that, upon being told of John Marshall's decision in Worcester v. Georgia, *he said: "John Marshall has made his decision, now let him enforce it." Georgia ignored the* Worcester *decision. Samuel Worcester remained in jail. President Jackson ordered the United States Army to expel the Cherokee Nation from Georgia and remove them to Indian Territory, present-day Oklahoma. In the winter of 1838 fifteen thousand Cherokee men, women, and children, many of whom died from exposure, disease, and starvation, were forced onto the Trail of Tears.*

THE NATIVE AMERICAN CASES
Elk v. Wilkins

*Every male person of the age of twenty-one years or up-
wards, belonging to either of the following classes, [First.
Citizens of the United States. Second. Persons of foreign
birth who have declared their intention to become citizens
. . .] who shall have resided in the State six months, and in
the county, precinct or ward for the term provided by
law, shall be an elector.*

The Nebraska Constitution

On April 6, 1880 John Elk, "an Indian, born within the
United States," and residing in the city of Omaha, Nebraska, for more than six months, attempted to register as a
voter and cast a vote in the general election for the Omaha City Council. Charles Wilkins, the Registrar of Omaha's Fifth Ward, refused to register Elk as a qualified voter, as defined by the Nebraska Constitution. Wilkins'
stated reason for denying to register Elk was that, as an
Indian, Elk was not a citizen of the United States.

John Elk, claiming that he had complied with all the legal
residence requirements for voters under the Nebraska
Constitution, sued Charles Wilkins for depriving him of
his right to vote on account of his race and color. The
suit, filed in the United States Court for the District of
Nebraska, charged that Wilkins had, "corruptly, willfully
and maliciously," violated Elk's rights under the Fourteenth and Fifteenth Amendments to the United States
Constitution. Elk asked for damages of $6,000 and the
right to register to vote. Wilkins argued that Elk, an Indian, was not a citizen of the United States and could not
sue him in a United States Court. The United States
Court for the District of Nebraska found for Wilkins and
Elk appealed to the United States Supreme Court.

On November 3, 1884 Justice Horace Gray announced the
7-2 decision of the Court. The edited text follows.

THE ELK COURT

Chief Justice Morrison Waite
Appointed by President Grant
Served 1874 - 1888

Associate Justice Samuel Miller
Appointed by President Lincoln
Served 1862 - 1890

Associate Justice Stephen Field
Appointed by President Lincoln
Served 1863 - 1897

Associate Justice Joseph Bradley
Appointed by President Grant
Served 1870 - 1892

Associate Justice John Marshall Harlan
Appointed by President Hayes
Served 1877 - 1911

Associate Justice William Woods
Appointed by President Hayes
Served 1880 - 1887

Associate Justice Stanley Matthews
Appointed by President Garfield
Served 1881 - 1889

Associate Justice Horace Gray
Appointed by President Arthur
Served 1881 - 1902

Associate Justice Samuel Blatchford
Appointed by President Arthur
Served 1882 - 1893

The unedited text of *Elk v. Wilkins* can be found on page 94, volume 112 of *United States Reports.*

ELK v. WILKINS
November 3, 1884

JUSTICE GRAY: The plaintiff [John Elk], in support of his action, relies on the first clause of the first section of the Fourteenth Article of Amendment of the Constitution of the United States, by which "all persons born or naturalized in the United States, and subject to the jurisdiction thereof, are citizens of the United States and of the State wherein they reside;" and on the Fifteenth Article of Amendment, which provides that "the right of citizens of the United States to vote shall not be denied or abridged by the United States or by any State on account of race, color, or previous condition of servitude."

. . . . [T]he only point argued by the defendant [Charles Wilkins] in this court is whether the petition sets forth facts enough to constitute a cause of action [a case].

The decision of this point . . . depends upon the question whether the legal conclusion, that under and by virtue of the Fourteenth Amendment of the Constitution [Elk] is a citizen of the United States, is supported by the facts . . . , to wit: [Elk] is an Indian, and was born in the United States, and has severed his tribal relation to the Indian tribes, and fully and completely surrendered himself to the jurisdiction of the United States, and still continues to be subject to the jurisdiction of the United States, and is a *bona fide* resident of the State of Nebraska and city of Omaha.

The petition, while it does not show of what Indian tribe [Elk] was a member, yet, by the allegations that he "is an Indian, and was born within the United States," and that "he had severed his tribal relation to the Indian tribes," clearly implies that he was born a member of one of the Indian tribes within the limits of the United States, which still exists and is recognized as a tribe by the government of the United States. Though [Elk] alleges that he "had fully and completely surrendered himself to the jurisdiction of the United States," he does not allege that the United States accepted his surrender, or that he has ever been naturalized, or taxed, or in any way recognized or treated as a citizen, by the State or by the United States. Nor is it contended by his counsel that there is any statute or treaty that makes him a citizen.

The question then is, whether an Indian, born a member of one of the Indian tribes within the United States, is, merely by reason of his birth within the United States, and of his afterwards voluntarily separating himself from his tribe and taking up his residence among white citizens, a citizen of the United States, within the meaning of the first section of the Fourteenth Amendment of the Constitution.

Under the Constitution of the United States, as originally established, "Indians not taxed" were excluded from the persons according to whose numbers representatives and direct taxes were apportioned among the several States; and Congress had and exercised the power to regulate commerce with the Indian tribes, and the members thereof, whether within or without the boundaries of one of the States of the Union. The Indian tribes, being within the territorial limits of the United States, were not, strictly speaking, foreign States; but they were alien nations, distinct political communities, with whom the United States might and habitually did deal, as they thought fit, either through treaties made by the President and Senate, or through acts of Congress in the ordinary forms of legislation. The members of those tribes owed immediate allegiance to their several tribes, and were not part of the people of the United States. They were in a dependent condition, a state of pupilage, resembling that of a ward to his guardian. Indians and their property, exempt from taxation by treaty or statute of the United States, could not be taxed by any State. General acts of Congress did not apply to Indians, unless so expressed as to clearly manifest an intention to include them.

The alien and dependent condition of the members of the Indian tribes could not be put off at their own will, without the action or assent of the United States. They were never deemed citizens of the United States, except under explicit provisions of treaty or statute to that effect, either declaring a certain tribe, or such members of it as chose to remain behind on the removal of the tribe westward, to be citizens, or authorizing individuals of particular tribes to become citizens on application to a court of the United States for naturalization, and satisfactory proof of fitness for civilized life; for examples of which see treaties in 1817 and 1835 with the Cherokees, and in 1820, 1825 and 1830 with the Choctaws; in 1855 with the Wyandotts; in 1861 and in March, 1866, with the Pottawatomies; in 1862 with the Ottawas; and the Kickapoos; and acts of Congress of March 3, 1989, concerning the Brothertown Indians, and of March 3, 1843, and March 3, 1865, concerning the Stockbridge Indians.

Chief Justice Taney, in the passage cited for the plaintiff [Dred Scott] from his opinion in *Scott v. Sandford*, did not affirm [uphold] or imply that either the Indian tribes, or individual members of those tribes, had the right, beyond other foreigners, to become citizens of their own will, without being naturalized by the United States. His words were: "They" (the Indian tribes) "may, without doubt, like the subjects of any foreign government, be naturalized by the authority of Congress, and become citizens of a State, and of the United States; and if an individual should leave his nation or tribe, and take up his abode among the white population, he would be entitled to all the rights and privileges which would belong to an emigrant from any other foreign people." But an emigrant from any foreign State cannot become a citizen of the United States without a formal renunciation of his old allegiance, and an acceptance by the United States of that renunciation through such form of naturalization as may be required by law.

The distinction between citizenship by birth and citizenship by naturalization is clearly marked in the provisions of the Constitution, by which "no person, except a natural born citizen, or a citizen of the United States at the time of the adoption of this Constitution, shall be eligible to the office of President;" and "the Congress shall have power to establish an uniform rule of naturalization."

By the Thirteenth Amendment of the Constitution slavery was prohibited. The main object of the opening sentence of the Fourteenth Amendment was to settle the question, upon which there had been a difference of opinion throughout the country and in this court, as to the citizenship of free negroes (*Scott v. Sandford*); and to put it beyond doubt that all persons, white or black, and whether formerly slaves or not, born or naturalized in the United States, and owing no allegiance to any alien power, should be citizens of the United States and of the State in which they reside.

This section contemplates two sources of citizenship, and two sources only: birth and naturalization. The persons declared to be citizens are "all persons born or naturalized in the United States, and subject to the jurisdiction thereof." The evident meaning of these last words is, not merely subject in some respect or degree to the jurisdiction of the United States, but completely subject to their political jurisdiction, and owing them direct and immediate allegiance. And the words relate to the time of birth in the one case, as they do to the time of naturalization in the other. Persons not thus subject to the jurisdiction of the United States at the time of birth cannot become so afterwards, except by being naturalized, either individually, as by proceedings under the naturalization acts, or collectively, as by the force of a treaty by which foreign territory is acquired.

Indians born within the territorial limits of the United States, members of, and owing immediate allegiance to, one of the Indian tribes (an alien, though dependent, power), although in a geographical sense born in the United States, are no more "born in the United States and subject to the jurisdiction thereof," within the meaning of the first section of the Fourteenth Amendment, than the children of subjects of any foreign government born within the domain of that government, or the children born within the United States, of ambassadors or other public ministers of foreign nations.

This view is confirmed by the second section of the Fourteenth Amendment, which provides that "representatives shall be apportioned among the several States according to their respective numbers, counting the whole number of persons in each State, excluding Indians not taxed." Slavery having been abolished, and the persons formerly held

as slaves made citizens, this clause fixing the apportionment of representatives has abrogated so much of the corresponding clause of the original Constitution as counted
only three-fifths of such persons. But Indians not taxed
are still excluded from the count, for the reason that they
are not citizens. Their absolute exclusion from the basis
of representation, in which all other persons are now included, is wholly inconsistent with their being considered
citizens.

So the further provision of the second section for a pro-
portionate reduction of the basis of the representation of
any State in which the right to vote for presidential electors, representatives in Congress, or executive or judicial
officers or members of the legislature of a State, is denied,
except for participation in rebellion or other crime, to
"any of the male inhabitants of such State, being twenty-
one years of age and citizens of the United States," cannot
apply to a denial of the elective franchise to Indians not
taxed, who form no part of the people entitled to representation.

It is also worthy of remark, that the language used, about
the same time, by the very Congress which framed the
Fourteenth Amendment, in the first section of the Civil
Rights Act of April 9, 1866, declaring who shall be citizens of the United States, is "all persons born in the United States, and not subject to any foreign power, excluding
Indians not taxed."

Such Indians, then, not being citizens by birth, can only
become citizens in the second way mentioned in the Fourteenth Amendment, by being "naturalized in the United
States," by or under some treaty or statute.

The action of the political departments of the government, not only after the proposal of the Amendment by Congress to the States in June, 1866, but since the proclamation in July, 1868, of its ratification by the requisite number of States, accords with this construction.

While the Amendment was pending before the legislatures of the several States, treaties containing provisions for the naturalization of members of Indian tribes as citizens of the United States were made on July 4, 1866, with the Delawares, in 1867 with various tribes in Kansas, and with the Pottawatomies, and in April, 1868, with the Sioux.

The treaty of 1867 with the Kansas Indians strikingly illustrates the principle that no one can become a citizen of a nation without its consent, and directly contradicts the supposition that a member of an Indian tribe can at will be alternately a citizen of the United States and a member of the tribe.

That treaty not only provided for the naturalization of members of the Ottawa, Miami, Peoria, and other tribes, and their families, upon their making declaration, before the District Court of the United States, of their intention to become citizens; but, after reciting that some of the Wyandotts, who had become citizens under the treaty of 1855, were "unfitted for the responsibilities of citizenship;" and enacting that a register of the whole people of this tribe, resident in Kansas or elsewhere, should be taken, under the direction of the Secretary of the Interior, showing the names of "all who declare their desire to be and remain Indians and in a tribal condition," and of incompetents and orphans as described in the treaty of 1855, and that such persons, and those only, should thereafter constitute the tribe; it provided that "no one who has heretofore consented to become a citizen, nor the wife or children of any such person, shall be allowed to become members of the tribe, except by the free consent of the tribe after its new organization, and unless the agent shall certify that such party is, through poverty or incapacity, unfit to continue in the exercise of the responsibilities of citizenship of the United States, and likely to become a public charge."

Since the ratification of the Fourteenth Amendment, Congress has passed several acts for naturalizing Indians of certain tribes, which would have been superfluous if they were, or might become, without any action of the government, citizens of the United States.

. . . . The national legislation has tended more and more towards the education and civilization of the Indians, and fitting them to be citizens. But the question whether any Indian tribes, or any members thereof, have become so far advanced in civilization, that they should be let out of the state of pupilage, and admitted to the privileges and responsibilities of citizenship, is a question to be decided by the nation whose wards they are and whose citizens they seek to become, and not by each Indian for himself.

There is nothing in the statutes or decisions, referred to by counsel, to control the conclusion to which we have been brought by a consideration of the language of the Fourteenth Amendment, and of the condition of the Indians at the time of its proposal and ratification.

. . . . The law upon the question before us has been well stated by Judge Deady in the District Court of the United States for the District of Oregon. In giving judgment against the plaintiff in a case resembling [this one], he said: "Being born a member of 'an independent political community' - the Chinook - he was not born subject to the jurisdiction of the United States - not born in its allegiance." And in a later case he said: "But an Indian cannot make himself a citizen of the United States without the consent and co-operation of the government. The fact that he has abandoned his nomadic life or tribal relations, and adopted the habits and manners of civilized people, may be a good reason why he should be made a citizen of the United States, but does not of itself make him one. To be a citizen of the United States is a political privilege which no one, not born to, can assume without its consent in some form. The Indians in Oregon, not being born subject to the jurisdiction of the United States, were not born citizens thereof, and I am not aware of any law or treaty by which any of them have been made so since."

Upon the question whether any action of a State can confer rights of citizenship on Indians of a tribe still recognized by the United States as retaining its tribal existence, we need not, and do not, express an opinion, because the State of Nebraska is not shown to have taken any action affecting the condition of [Elk].

[Elk], not being a citizen of the United States under the Fourteenth Amendment of the Constitution, has been deprived of no right secured by the Fifteenth Amendment, and cannot maintain this action. Judgment affirmed.

The Fourteenth Amendment's Citizenship Clause reads in full: "All persons born or naturalized in the United States, and subject to the jurisdiction thereof, are citizens of the United States and of the state wherein they reside." The

Elk Court excluded Native Americans from this definition of citizenship. Not until 1924 did the United States Congress declare all Native Americans to be United States citizens.

THE FUGITIVE SLAVE CASES

Prigg v. Pennsylvania

No person held to service or labor in one state, under the laws thereof, escaping to another shall, in consequence of any law or regulation therein, be discharged from such service or labor, but shall be delivered up on claim of the party to whom such service or labor may be due.

The Constitution's Fugitive Slave Clause

The first Fugitive Slave Act, passed by Congress on February 12, 1793, provided for the return of runaway slaves from one state to another in accordance with Article IV, Section II, Clause III of the Constitution, known as the Fugitive Slave Clause. The Pennsylvania Personal Liberty Law, enacted March 26, 1826, provided that, contrary to the Fugitive Slave Act, no runaway slaves could be forced to leave Pennsylvania against their will and be returned to a state where they would be again held as slaves.

In 1832 Margaret Morgan escaped from Maryland where she was held as a slave and fled to Pennsylvania under whose laws she was free. In 1837 Edward Prigg, a slave-catcher from Maryland in the employ of Morgan's former owner, found and captured her and, in accordance with the Fugitive Slave Act, requested a Pennsylvania Court to order her return to Maryland. The Court refused. Prigg then returned both Morgan, and her Pennsylvania-born children, to Maryland. Edward Prigg was indicted in Pennsylvania for kidnapping. A York County jury found him guilty of a violation of the Pennsylvania Personal Liberty Law which carried a penalty of seven to twenty-one years at hard labor. Prigg appealed his conviction to the Pennsylvania Supreme Court which upheld his guilt. Prigg then appealed to the United States Supreme Court.

On March 1, 1842 Justice Joseph Story announced the 9-0 decision of the Court. The edited text follows.

THE PRIGG COURT

Chief Justice Roger Brooke Taney
Appointed by President Jackson
Served 1836 - 1864

Associate Justice Joseph Story
Appointed by President Madison
Served 1811 - 1845

Associate Justice Smith Thompson
Appointed by President Monroe
Served 1823 - 1843

Associate Justice John McLean
Appointed by President Jackson
Served 1829 - 1861

Associate Justice Henry Baldwin
Appointed by President Jackson
Served 1830 - 1844

Associate Justice James Wayne
Appointed by President Jackson
Served 1835 - 1867

Associate Justice John Catron
Appointed by President Jackson
Served 1837 - 1865

Associate Justice John McKinley
Appointed by President Van Buren
Served 1837 - 1852

Associate Justice Peter Daniel
Appointed by President Van Buren
Served 1841 - 1860

The unedited text of *Prigg v. Pennsylvania* can be found on page 593, volume 41 of *United States Reports.*

PRIGG v. PENNSYLVANIA
March 1, 1842

JUSTICE STORY: This is [an appeal] to the supreme court of Pennsylvania . . . for the purpose of revising the judgment of that court, in a case involving the construction of the constitution and laws of the United States. The facts are briefly these:

The plaintiff [Edward Prigg] was indicted [charged] in . . . York county [court], for having, with force and violence, taken and carried away from that county, to the state of Maryland, a certain negro woman, named Margaret Morgan, with a design and intention of selling and disposing of, and keeping her, as a slave or servant for life, contrary to a statute of Pennsylvania [the Liberty Law], passed on the 26th of March 1826. That statute, in the first section, in substance, provides, that if any person or persons shall, from and after the passing of the act, by force and violence, take and carry away, or cause to be taken and carried away, and shall, by fraud or false pretense, seduce, or cause to be seduced, or shall attempt to take, carry away or seduce, any negro or mulatto, from any part of that commonwealth, with a design and intention of selling and disposing of, or causing to be sold, or of keeping and detaining, or of causing to be kept and detained, such negro or mulatto, as a slave or servant for life, or for any term whatsoever; every such person or persons, his or their aiders or abettors, 'shall, on conviction thereof, be deemed guilty of felony, and shall forfeit and pay a sum not less than five hundred, nor more than one thousand dollars; and moreover, shall be sentenced to undergo servitude for any term or terms of years, not less than seven years nor exceeding twenty-one years; and shall be confined and kept to hard labor. . . .

[Edward Prigg] pleaded not guilty to the indictment; and
at the trial, the jury found a special verdict, which, in substance, states, that the negro woman, Margaret Morgan,
was a slave for life, and held to labor and service under
and according to the laws of Maryland, to a certain Margaret Ashmore, a citizen of Maryland; that the slave escaped and fled from Maryland, into Pennsylvania, in
1832; that [Prigg], being legally constituted the agent and
attorney of the said Margaret Ashmore, in 1837, caused
the said negro woman to be taken and apprehended as a
fugitive from labor, by a state constable, under a warrant
[an order] from a Pennsylvania magistrate; that the said
negro woman was thereupon brought before the said magistrate, who refused to take further cognisance of the
case; and thereupon, [Prigg] did remove, take and carry
away the said negro woman and her children, out of Pennsylvania, into Maryland, and did deliver the said negro
woman and her children into the custody and possession
of the said Margaret Ashmore. The special verdict further finds, that one of the children was born in Pennsylvania, more than a year after the said negro woman had fled
and escaped from Maryland. Upon this special verdict,
the court . . . of York County adjudged that [Prigg] was
guilty of the offence charged in the indictment. A[n ap-
peal] was brought from that judgment to the supreme
court of Pennsylvania, where the judgment was, *pro for-
ma* [as a matter of form], affirmed [upheld]. From this
latter judgment, the present [appeal] has been brought to
this court.

. . . . The question arising in the case, as to the constitutionality of the [Liberty Law] of Pennsylvania, has been
most elaborately argued at the bar. The counsel for
[Prigg] have contended, that the statute of Pennsylvania is
unconstitutional; first, because congress has the exclusive

power of legislation upon the subject-matter, under the constitution of the United States, and under the [Fugitive Slave Act of 1793], which was passed in pursuance thereof; secondly, that if this power is not exclusive in congress, still the concurrent power of the state legislatures is suspended by the actual exercise of the power of congress; and thirdly, that if not suspended, still the statute of Pennsylvania, in all its provisions applicable to this case, is in direct collision with the act of congress, and therefore, is unconstitutional and void. The counsel for Pennsylvania maintain the negative of all these points.

Few questions which have ever come before this court involve more delicate and important considerations; and few upon which the public at large may be presumed to feel a more profound and pervading interest. We have accordingly given them our most deliberate examination; and it has become my duty to state the result to which we have arrived, and the reasoning by which it is supported.

Before, however, we proceed to the points more immediately before us, it may be well, in order to clear the case of difficulty, to say, that in the exposition of this part of the constitution, we shall limit ourselves to those considerations which appropriately and exclusively belong to it, without laying down any rules of interpretation of a more general nature. It will, indeed, probably, be found, when we look to the character of the constitution itself, the objects which it seeks to attain, the powers which it confers, the duties which it enjoins [commands], and the rights which it secures, as well as the known historical fact, that many of its provisions were matters of compromise of opposing interests and opinions, that no uniform rule of interpretation can be applied to it, which may not allow, even if it does not positively demand, many modifications, in its actual application to particular clauses. And, perhaps, the safest rule of interpretation, after all, will be found to be to look to the nature and objects of the particular powers, duties and rights, with all the lights and aids of contemporary history; and to give to the words of each just such operation and force, consistent with their legitimate meaning, as may fairly secure and attain the ends proposed.

There are two clauses in the constitution upon the subject of fugitives, which stands in juxtaposition with each other, and have been thought mutually to illustrate each other. They are both contained in the second section of the fourth article, and are in the following words: "A person charged in any state with treason, felony or other crime, who shall flee from justice, and be found in another state, shall, on demand of the executive authority of the state from which he fled, be delivered up, to be removed to the state having jurisdiction of the crime." "No person held to service or labor in one state, under the laws thereof, escaping into another, shall, in consequence of any law or regulation therein, be discharged from such service or labor; but shall be delivered up, on claim of the party to whom such service or labor may be due."

The last clause is that, the true interpretation whereof is directly in judgment before us. Historically, it is well known, that the object of this clause was to secure to the citizens of the slave-holding states the complete right and title of ownership in their slaves, as property, in every state in the Union into which they might escape from the state where they were held in servitude. The full recognition of this right and title was indispensable to the security of this species of property in all the slave-holding states; and, indeed, was so vital to the preservation of their

domestic interests and institutions, that it cannot be doubted, that it constituted a fundamental article, without the
adoption of which the Union could not have been formed.
Its true design was, to guard against the doctrines and
principles prevalent in the non-slave-holding states, by
preventing them from intermeddling with, or obstructing,
or abolishing the rights of the owners of slaves.

By the general law of nations, no nation is bound to recog-
nise the state of slavery, as to foreign slaves found within
its territorial dominions, when it is in opposition to its
own policy and institutions, in favor of the subjects of
other nations where slavery is recognised. If it does it, it
is as a matter of comity [respect], and not as a matter of
international right. The state of slavery is deemed to be a
mere municipal regulation, founded upon and limited to
the range of the territorial laws. . . . It is manifest, from
this consideration, that if the constitution had not contained this clause, every non-slave-holding state in the Union would have been at liberty to have declared free all
runaway slaves coming within its limits, and to have given
them entire immunity and protection against the claims of
their masters; a course which would have created the most
bitter animosities, and engendered perpetual strife between the different states. The clause was, therefore, of
the last importance to the safety and security of the
southern states, and could not have been surrendered by
them, without endangering their whole property in slaves.
The clause was accordingly adopted into the constitution,
by the unanimous consent of the framers of it; a proof at
once of its intrinsic and practical necessity.

How, then, are we to interpret the language of the clause?
The true answer is, in such a manner as, consistently with
the words, shall fully and completely effectuate the whole

objects of it. If, by one mode of interpretation, the right must become shadowy and unsubstantial, and without any remedial power adequate to the end, and by another mode, it will attain its just end and secure its manifest purpose, it would seem, upon principles of reasoning, absolutely irresistible, that the latter ought to prevail. No court of justice can be authorized so to construe [interpret] any clause of the constitution as to defeat its obvious ends, when another construction, equally accordant with the words and sense thereof, will enforce and protect them.

The clause manifestly contemplates the existence of a positive, unqualified right on the part of the owner of the slave, which no state law or regulation can in any way qualify, regulate, control or restrain. The slave is not to be discharged from service or labor, in consequence of any state law or regulation. Now, certainly, without indulging in any nicety of criticism upon words, it may fairly and reasonably be said, that any state law or state regulation, which interrupts, limits, delays or postpones the right of the owner to the immediate possession of the slave, and the immediate command of his service and labor, operates, *pro tanto* [as far as it goes], a discharge of the slave therefrom. The question can never be, how much the slave is discharged from; but whether he is discharged from any, by the natural or necessary operation of state laws or state regulations. The question is not one of quantity or degree, but of withholding or controlling the incidents of a positive and absolute right.

We have said, that the clause contains a positive and unqualified recognition of the right of the owner in the slave, unaffected by any state law or legislation whatsoever, because there is no qualification or restriction of it to be found therein; and we have no right to insert any, which is not expressed, and cannot be fairly implied. Especially, are we estopped [prevented] from so doing, when the clause puts the right to the service or labor upon the same ground, and to the same extent, in every other state as in the state from which the slave escaped, and in which he was held to the service or labor. If this be so, then all the incidents to that right attach also. The owner must, therefore, have the right to seize and repossess the slave, which the local laws of his own state confer upon him, as property; and we all know that this right of seizure and recaption is universally acknowledged in all the slave-holding states. Indeed, this is no more than a mere affirmance of the principles of the common law [law established by custom] applicable to this very subject. Justice Blackstone lays it down as unquestionable doctrine. "Recaption or reprisal (says he) is another species of remedy by the mere act of the party injured. This happens, when any one hath deprived another of his property in goods or chattels personal, or wrongfully detains one's wife, child or servant; in which case, the owner of the goods, and the husband, parent or master, may lawfully claim and retake them, wherever he happens to find them, so it be not in a riotous manner, or attended with a breach of the peace." Upon this ground, we have not the slightest hesitation in holding, that under and in virtue of the constitution, the owner of a slave is clothed with entire authority, in every state in the Union, to seize and recapture his slave, whenever he can do it, without any breach of the peace or any illegal violence. In this sense, and to this extent, this clause of the constitution may properly be said to execute itself, and to require no aid from legislation, state or national.

But the clause of the constitution does not stop here; nor, indeed, consistently with its professed objects, could it do

so. Many cases must arise, in which, if the remedy of the
owner were confined to the mere right of seizure and recaption, he would be utterly without any adequate redress.
He may not be able to lay his hands upon the slave. He
may not be able to enforce his rights against persons, who
either secrete or conceal, or withhold the slave. He may
be restricted by local legislation, as to the mode of proofs
of his ownership; as to the courts in which he shall sue,
and as to the actions which he may bring; or the process
he may use to compel the delivery of the slave. Nay! the
local legislation may be utterly inadequate to furnish the
appropriate redress, by authorizing no process *in rem*
[against the thing], or no specific mode of repossessing
the slave, leaving the owner, at best, not that right which
the constitution designed to secure, a specific delivery and
repossession of the slave, but a mere remedy in damages;
and that, perhaps, against persons utterly insolvent or
worthless. The state legislation may be entirely silent on
the whole subject, and its ordinary remedial process
framed with different views and objects; and this may be
innocently as well as designedly done, since every state is
perfectly competent, and has the exclusive right, to prescribe the remedies in its own judicial tribunals, to limit
the time as well as the mode of redress, and to deny jurisdiction over cases, which its own policy and its own institutions either prohibit or discountenance. If, therefore,
the clause of the constitution had stopped at the mere recognition of the right, without providing or contemplating
any means by which it might be established and enforced,
in cases where it did not execute itself, it is plain, that it
would have been, in a great variety of cases, a delusive
and empty annunciation. If it did not contemplate any action, either through state or national legislation, as auxil-
iaries to its more perfect enforcement in the form of
remedy, or of protection, then, as there would be no duty

on either to aid the right, it would be left to the mere comity of the states, to act as they should please, and would depend for its security upon the changing course of public opinion, the mutations of public policy, and the general adaptations of remedies for purposes strictly according to the *lex fori* [the law of the state where the suit is brought].

And this leads to the consideration of the other part of the clause, which implies at once a guarantee and duty. It says, "but he (the slave) shall be delivered up, on claim of the party to whom such service or labor may be due." Now, we think it exceedingly difficult, if not impracticable, to read this language, and not to feel, that it contemplated some further remedial redress than that which might be administered at the hands of the owner himself. A claim is to be made! What is a claim? It is, in a just juridical sense, a demand of some matter, as of right, made by one person upon another, to do or to forbear to do some act or thing as a matter of duty. A more limited, but at the same time, an equally expressive, definition was given by Lord Dyer, as cited in *Stowel v. Zouch*, and it is equally applicable to the present case: that "a claim is a challenge by a man of the propriety or ownership of a thing, which he has not in possession, but which is wrongfully detained from him." The slave is to be delivered up on the claim. By whom to be delivered up? In what mode to be delivered up? How, if a refusal takes place, is the right of delivery to be enforced? Upon what proofs? What shall be the evidence of a rightful recaption or delivery? When and under what circumstances shall the possession of the owner, after it is obtained, be conclusive of his right, so as to preclude any further inquiry or examination into it by local tribunals or otherwise, while the slave, in possession of the owner, is *in transitu* [on the

way] to the state from which he fled? These and many
other questions will readily occur upon the slightest attention to the clause; and it is obvious, that they can receive
but one satisfactory answer. They require the aid of legislation, to protect the right, to enforce the delivery, and to
secure the subsequent possession of the slave. If, indeed,
the constitution guaranties the right, and if it requires the
delivery upon the claim of the owner (as cannot well be
doubted), the natural inference certainly is, that the national government is clothed with the appropriate authority and functions to enforce it. The fundamental principle,
applicable to all cases of this sort, would seem to be, that
where the end is required, the means are given; and where
the duty is enjoined, the ability to perform it is contemplated to exist, on the part of the functionaries to whom it
is intrusted. The clause is found in the national constitution, and not in that of any state. It does not point out
any state functionaries, or any state action, to carry its
provisions into effect. The states cannot, therefore, be
compelled to enforce them; and it might well be deemed
an unconstitutional exercise of the power of interpretation, to insist, that the states are bound to provide means
to carry into effect the duties of the national government,
nowhere delegated or intrusted to them by the constitution. On the contrary, the natural, if not the necessary,
conclusion is, that the national government, in the absence
of all positive provisions to the contrary, is bound,
through its own proper departments, legislative, judicial
or executive, as the case may require, to carry into effect
all the rights and duties imposed upon it by the constitution. The remark of Mr. [James] Madison, in the *Federal-
ist* (No. 43), would seem in such cases to apply with peculiar force. "A right (says he) implies a remedy; and where
else would the remedy be deposited, than where it is de-

posited by the constitution?" meaning, as the contest shows, in the government of the United States.

It is plain, then, that where a claim is made by the owner, out of possession, for the delivery of a slave, it must be made, if at all, against some other person; and inasmuch as the right is a right of property, capable of being recognised and asserted by proceedings before a court of justice, between parties adverse to each other, it constitutes, in the strictest sense, a controversy between the parties, and a case "arising under the constitution" of the United States, within the express delegation of judicial power given by that instrument. Congress, then, may call that power into activity, for the very purpose of giving effect to that right; and if so, then it may prescribe the mode and extent in which it shall be applied, and how, and under what circumstances, the proceedings shall afford a complete protection and guarantee to the right.

Congress has taken this very view of the power and duty of the national government. As early as the year 1791, the attention of congress was drawn to it (as we shall hereafter more fully see), in consequence of some practical difficulties arising under the other clause, respecting fugitives from justice escaping into other states. The result of their deliberations was the passage of the act of the 12th of February 1793, which, after having, in the first and second sections, provided by the case of fugitives from justice, by a demand to be made of the delivery, through the executive authority of the state where they are found, proceeds, in the third section, to provide, that when a person held to labor or service in any of the United States, shall escape into any other of the states or territories, the person to whom such labor or service may be due, his agent or attorney, is hereby empowered to seize

or arrest such fugitive from labor, and take him or her before any judge of the circuit or district courts of the United States, residing or being within the state, or before any
magistrate of a county, city or town corporate, wherein
such seizure or arrest shall be made; and upon proof, to
the satisfaction of such judge or magistrate, either by oral
evidence or affidavit, that the person so seized or arrested,
doth, under the laws of the state or territory from which
he or she fled, owe service or labor to the person claiming
him or her, it shall be the duty of such judge or magistrate, to give a certificate thereof to such claimant, his
agent or attorney, which shall be sufficient warrant for
removing the said fugitive from labor, to the state or territory from which he or she fled. The fourth section provides a penalty against any person, who shall knowingly
and willingly obstruct or hinder such claimant, his agent
or attorney, in so seizing or arresting such fugitive from
labor, or rescue such fugitive from the claimant, or his
agent or attorney, when so arrested, or who shall harbor
or conceal such fugitive, after notice that he is such; and
it also saves to the person claiming such labor or service
his right of action for or on account of such injuries.

In a general sense, this act may be truly said to cover the
whole ground of the constitution, both as to fugitives
from justice, and fugitive slaves; that is, it covers both the
subjects, in its enactments; not because it exhausts the
remedies which may be applied by congress to enforce the
rights, if the provisions of the act shall in practice be
found not to attain the object of the constitution; but because it points out fully all the modes of attaining those
objects, which congress, in their discretion, have as yet
deemed expedient or proper to meet the exigencies of the
constitution. If this be so, then it would seem, upon just
principles of construction, that the legislation of congress,

if constitutional, must supersede all state legislation upon
the same subject; and by necessary implication prohibit it.
For, if congress have a constitutional power to regulate a
particular subject, and they do actually regulate it in a
given manner, and in a certain form, it cannot be, that the
state legislatures have a right to interfere, and as it were,
by way of compliment to the legislation of congress, to
prescribe additional regulations, and what they may deem
auxiliary provisions for the same purpose. In such a case,
the legislation of congress, in what it does prescribe, manifestly indicates, that it does not intend that there shall be
any further legislation to act upon the subject-matter. Its
silence as to what it does not do, is as expressive of what
its intention is, as the direct provisions made by it. This
doctrine was fully recognised by this court, in the case of
Houston v. Moore, where it was expressly held, that where
congress have exercised a power over a particular subject
given them by the constitution, it is not competent for
state legislation to add to the provisions of congress upon
that subject; for that the will of congress upon the whole
subject is as clearly established by what it has not declared, as by what it has expressed.

But it has been argued, that the act of congress is unconstitutional, because it does not fall within the scope of any
of the enumerated powers of legislation confided to that
body; and therefore, it is void. Stripped of its artificial
and technical structure, the argument comes to this, that
although rights are exclusively secured by, or duties are
exclusively imposed upon, the national government, yet,
unless the power to enforce these rights or to execute
these duties, can be found among the the express powers
of legislation enumerated in the constitution, they remain
without any means of giving them effect by any act of
congress; and they must operate solely *proprio vigore* [by

its own force], however defective may be their operation; nay! even although, in a practical sense, they may become a nullity, from the want of a proper remedy to enforce them, or to provide against their violation. If this be the true interpretation of the constitution, it must, in a great measure, fail to attain many of its avowed and positive objects, as a security of rights, and a recognition of duties. Such a limited construction of the constitution has never yet been adopted as correct, either in theory or practice. No one has ever supposed, that congress could, constitutionally, by its legislation, exercise powers, or enact laws, beyond the powers delegated to it by the constitution. But it has, on various occasions, exercised powers which were necessary and proper as means to carry into effect rights expressly given, and duties expressly enjoined thereby. The end being required, it has been deemed a just and necessary implication, that the means to accomplish it are given also; or, in other words, that the power flows as a necessary means to accomplish the end.

Thus, for example, although the constitution has declared, that representatives shall be apportioned among the states according to their respective federal numbers; and for this purpose, it has expressly authorized congress, by law, to provide for an enumeration of the population every ten years; yet the power to apportion representatives, after this enumeration is made, is nowhere found among the express powers given to congress, but it has always been acted upon, as irresistibly flowing from the duty positively enjoined by the constitution. Treaties made between the United States and foreign powers, often contain special provisions, which do not execute themselves, but require the interposition of congress to carry them into effect, and congress has constantly, in such cases, legislated on the subject; yet, although the power is given to the executive, with the consent of the senate, to make treaties, the power is nowhere in positive terms conferred upon congress to make laws to carry the stipulations of treaties into effect; it has been supposed to result from the duty of the national government to fulfil all the obligations of treaties. The senators and representatives in congress are, in all cases, except treason, felony and breach of the peace, exempted from arrest, during their attendance at the sessions thereof, and in going to and returning from the same. May not congress enforce this right, by authorizing a writ of *habeas corpus* [an order bringing someone before a court], to free them from an illegal arrest, in violation of this clause of the constitution? If it may not, then the specific remedy to enforce it must exclusively depend upon the local legislation of the states; and may be granted or refused, according to their own varying policy or pleasure. The constitution also declares, that the privilege of the writ of *habeas corpus* shall not be suspended, unless, when in cases of rebellion or invasion, the public safety may require it. No express power is given to congress to secure this invaluable right in the non-enumerated cases, or to suspend the writ in cases of rebellion or invasion. And yet it would be difficult to say, since this great writ of liberty is usually provided for by the ordinary functions of legislation, and can be effectually provided for only in this way, that it ought not to be deemed, by necessary implication, within the scope of the legislative power of congress. These cases are put merely by way of illustration, to show, that the rule of interpretation, insisted upon at the argument, is quite too narrow to provide for the ordinary exigencies of the national government, in cases where rights are intended to be absolutely secured, and duties are positively enjoined by the constitution.

The very act of 1793, now under consideration, affords the most conclusive proof, that congress has acted upon a very different rule of interpretation, and has supposed, that the right as well as the duty of legislation on the subject of fugitives from justice, and fugitive slaves, was within the scope of the constitutional authority conferred on the national legislature. In respect to fugitives from justice, the constitution, although it expressly provides, that the demand shall be made by the executive authority of the state from which the fugitive has fled, is silent as to the party upon whom the demand is to be made, and as to the mode in which it shall be made. This very silence occasioned embarrassments in enforcing the right and duty, at an early period after the adoption of the constitution; and produced a hesitation on the part of the executive authority of Virginia to deliver up a fugitive from justice, upon the demand of the executive of Pennsylvania, in the year 1791; and as we historically know from the message of President Washington, and the public documents of that period, it was the immediate cause of the passing of the act of 1793, which designated the person (the state executive) upon whom the demand should be made, and the mode and proofs upon and in which it should be made. From that time down to the present hour, not a doubt has been breathed upon the constitutionality of this part of the act; and every executive in the Union has constantly acted upon and admitted its validity. Yet the right and the duty are dependent, as to their mode of execution, solely on the act of congress; and but for that, they would remain a nominal right and passive duty, the execution of which being intrusted to and required of no one in particular, all persons might be at liberty to disregard it. This very acquiescence, under such circumstances, of the highest state functionaries, is a most decisive proof of the universality of the opinion, that the act

is founded in a just construction of the constitution, independent of the vast influence, which it ought to have as a
contemporaneous exposition of the provisions, by those
who were its immediate framers, or intimately connected
with its adoption.

The same uniformity of acquiescence in the validity of
the act of 1793, upon the other part of the subject-matter,
that of fugitive slaves, has prevailed throughout the whole
Union, until a comparatively recent period. Nay! being
from its nature and character more readily susceptible of
being brought into controversy in courts of justice, than
the former, and of enlisting in opposition to it, the feelings, and it may be, the prejudices, of some portions of the
non-slave-holding states, it has naturally been brought under adjudication in several states in the Union, and particularly in Massachusetts, New York and Pennsylvania; and
on all these occasions its validity has been affirmed. . . .
So far as the judges of the courts of the United States
have been called upon to enforce it, and to grant the certificate required by it, it is believed, that it has been uniformly recognised as a binding and valid law, and as imposing a constitutional duty. Under such circumstances, if
the question were one of doubtful construction, such long
acquiescence in it, such contemporaneous expositions of it,
and such extensive and uniform recognition of its validity,
would, in our judgment, entitle the question to be considered at rest; unless, indeed, the interpretation of the constitution is to be delivered over to interminable doubt
throughout the whole progress of legislation and of national operations. Congress, the executive, and the judiciary, have, upon various occasions, acted upon this as a
sound and reasonable doctrine. . . .

But we do not wish to rest our present opinion upon the
ground either of contemporaneous exposition, or long acquiescence, or even practical action; neither do we mean
to admit the question to be of a doubtful nature, and
therefore, as properly calling for the aid of such considerations. On the contrary, our judgment would be the same,
if the question were entirely new, and the act of congress
were of recent enactment. We hold the act to be clearly
constitutional, in all its leading provisions, and, indeed,
with the exception of that part which confers authority
upon state magistrates, to be free from reasonable doubt
and difficulty, upon the grounds already stated. As to the
authority so conferred upon state magistrates, while a difference of opinion has existed, and may exist still, on the
point, in different states, whether state magistrates are
bound to act under it, none is entertained by this court,
that state magistrates may, if they choose, exercise that authority, unless prohibited by state legislation.

The remaining question is, whether the power of legislation upon this subject is exclusive in the national government, or concurrent in the states, until it is exercised by
congress. In our opinion, it is exclusive; and we shall now
proceed briefly to state our reasons for that opinion. The
doctrine stated by this court, in *Sturges v. Crowninshield*,
contains the true, although not the sole, rule or consideration, which is applicable to this particular subject.
"Wherever," said Chief Justice Marshall, in delivering the
opinion of the court, "the terms in which a power is granted to congress, or the nature of the power, require, that it
should be exercised exclusively by congress, the subject is
as completely taken from the state legislatures, as if they
had been forbidden to act." The nature of the power, and
the true objects to be attained by it, are then as important

to be weighed, in considering the question of its exclusiveness, as the words in which it is granted.

In the first place, it is material to state (what has been already incidentally hinted at), that the right to seize and retake fugitive slaves and the duty to deliver them up, in whatever state of the Union they may be found, and, of course, the corresponding power in congress to use the appropriate means to enforce the right and duty, derive their whole validity and obligation exclusively from the constitution of the United States, and are there, for the first time, recognised and established in that peculiar character. Before the adoption of the constitution, no state had any power whatsoever over the subject, except within its own territorial limits, and could not bind the sovereignty or the legislation of other states. Whenever the right was acknowledged, or the duty enforced, in any state, it was as a matter of comity [respect], and not as a matter of strict moral, political or international obligation or duty. Under the constitution, it is recognised as an absolute, positive right and duty, pervading the whole Union with an equal and supreme force, uncontrolled and uncontrollable by state sovereignty or state legislation. It is, therefore, in a just sense, a new and positive right, independent of comity, confined to no territorial limits, and bounded by no state institutions or policy. The natural inference deducible from this consideration certainly is, in the absence of any positive delegation of power to the state legislatures, that it belongs to the legislative department of the national government, to which it owes its origin and establishment. It would be a strange anomaly, and forced construction, to suppose, that the national government meant to rely for the due fulfilment of its own proper duties, and the rights it intended to secure, upon state legislation, and not upon that of the Union. A *fort-*

iori [with stronger reason], it would be more objectionable, to suppose, that a power, which was to be the same throughout the Union, should be confided to state sovereignty, which could not rightfully act beyond its own territorial limits.

In the next place, the nature of the provision and the objects to be attained by it, require that it should be controlled by one and the same will, and act uniformly by the same system of regulations throughout the Union. If, then, the states have a right, in the absence of legislation by congress, to act upon the subject, each state is at liberty to prescribe just such regulations as suit its own policy, local convenience and local feelings. The legislation of one state may not only be different from, but utterly repugnant to and incompatible with, that of another. The time and mode, and limitation of the remedy, the proofs of the title, and all other incidents applicable thereto, may be prescribed in one state, which are rejected or disclaimed in another. One state may require the owner to sue in one mode, another, in a different mode. One state may make a statute of limitations as to the remedy, in its own tribunals, short and summary; another may prolong the period, and yet restrict the proofs. Nay, some states may utterly refuse to act upon the subject at all; and others may refuse to open its courts to any remedies *in rem* [against the thing], because they would interfere with their own domestic policy, institutions or habits. The right, therefore, would never, in a practical sense, be the same in all the states. It would have no unity of purpose, or uniformity of operation. The duty might be enforced in some states; retarded or limited in others; and denied, as compulsory, in many, if not in all. Consequences like these must have been foreseen as very likely to occur in the non-slaveholding states, where legislation, if not silent on the subject, and purely voluntary, could scarcely be presumed to be favorable to the exercise of the rights of the owner.

It is scarcely conceivable, that the slave-holding states would have been satisfied with leaving to the legislation of the non-slave-holding states, a power of regulation, in the absence of that of congress, which would or might practically amount to a power to destroy the rights of the owner. If the argument, therefore, of a concurrent power in the states to act upon the subject-matter, in the absence of legislation by congress, be well founded; then, if congress had never acted at all, or if the act of congress should be repealed, without providing a substitute, there would be a resulting authority in each of the states to regulate the whole subject, at its pleasure, and to dole out its own remedial justice, or withhold it, at its pleasure, and according to its own views of policy and expediency. Surely, such a state of things never could have been intended, under such a solemn guarantee of right and duty. On the other hand, construe [interpret] the right of legislation as exclusive in congress, and every evil and every danger vanishes. The right and the duty are then co-extensive and uniform in remedy and operation throughout the whole Union. The owner has the same security, and the same remedial justice, and the same exemption from state regulation and control, through however many states he may pass with his fugitive slave in his possession, *in transitu* [on the way] to his own domicile. But upon the other supposition, the moment he passes the state line, he becomes amenable to the laws of another sovereignty, whose regulations may greatly embarrass or delay the exercise of his rights, and even be repugnant to those of the state where he first arrested the fugitive. Consequences like these show, that the nature and objects of the provisions imperiously require, that to make it effectual, it should be construed to be exclusive of state authority. We adopt the language of this court in *Sturges v. Crowninshield,* and say, that "it has never been supposed, that the concurrent power of legislation extended to every possible case in which its exercise by the states has not been expressly prohibited; the confusion of such a practice would be endless." And we know no case in which the confusion and public inconvenience and mischiefs thereof could be more completely exemplified than the present.

These are some of the reasons, but by no means all, upon which we hold the power of legislation on this subject to be exclusive in congress. To guard, however, against any possible misconstruction of our views, it is proper to state, that we are by no means to be understood, in any manner whatsoever, to doubt or to interfere with the police power belonging to the states, in virtue of their general sovereignty. That policy power extends over all subjects within territorial limits of the states, and has never been conceded to the United States. It is wholly distinguishable from the right and duty secured by the provision now under consideration; which is exclusively derived from and secured by the constitution of the United States, and owes its whole efficacy thereto. We entertain no doubt whatsoever, that the states, in virtue of their general police power, possesses full jurisdiction to arrest and restrain runaway slaves, and remove them from their borders, and otherwise to secure themselves against their depredations and evil example, as they certainly may do in cases of idlers, vagabonds and paupers. The rights of the owners of fugitive slaves are in no just sense interfered with, or regulated, by such a course; and in many cases, the operations of this police power, although designed generally for other purposes, for protection, safety and peace of the state, may essentially promote and aid the interests of the owners. But such regulations can never be permitted to interfere with, or to obstruct, the just rights of the owner to reclaim his slave, derived from the constitution of the United States, or with the remedies prescribed by congress to aid and enforce the same.

Upon these grounds, we are of opinion, that the act of Pennsylvania upon which this indictment is founded, is unconstitutional and void. It purports to punish as a public offence against that state, the very act of seizing and removing a slave, by his master, which the constitution of the United States was designed to justify and uphold. The special verdict finds this fact, and the state courts have rendered judgment against [Prigg] upon that verdict. That judgment must, therefore, be reversed, and the cause remanded [returned] to the supreme court of Pennsylvania, with directions to carry into effect the judgment of this court rendered upon the special verdict, in favor of [Prigg].

On June 28, 1864 the United States Congress approved the repeal of the Fugitive Slave Acts of 1793 and 1850. The repeal reads in full: "Be it enacted by the Senate and the House of Representatives of the United States of America in Congress assembled, That sections three and four of an act entitled 'An Act respecting fugitives from justice and persons escaping from the service of their masters,' passed February, seventeen hundred and ninety-three and an act to amend and supplementary to the act entitled 'An Act respecting fugitives from justice and persons escaping from the service of their masters,' passed February, seventeen hundred and ninety-three, passed September, eighteen hundred and fifty, and the same are hereby repealed."

THE FUGITIVE SLAVE CASES

Ableman v. Booth

This Constitution, and the laws of the United States which shall be made in pursuance thereof . . . shall be the supreme law of the land; and the Judges in every state shall be bound thereby, any thing in the Constitution or laws of any state to the contrary notwithstanding.

The Supremacy Clause
Article VI, Clause II

The Second Fugitive Slave Act, officially called *"An Act respecting Fugitives from Justice and Persons escaping from the service of their Masters,"* was enacted as part of the Compromise of 1850, and was approved by the Congress on September 18, 1850. Supplementing the Fugitive Slave Act of 1793, the Second Fugitive Slave Act provided federal assistance to slaveholders in the return of escaped slaves, allowed "reasonable force" to be used against runaway slaves, and provided penalties for those assisting them in their flight from slavery.

On March 11, 1854 Sherman M. Booth, an abolitionist, was charged with aiding and abetting the escape of a fugitive slave from federal custody in Milwaukee, Wisconsin. U.S. Marshall Stephen Ableman arrested Booth for violating the Fugitive Slave Act. Booth, asserting that the Fugitive Slave Act was unconstitutional, petitioned Wisconsin Supreme Court Justice A.D. Smith to free him. Booth was freed. Ableman appealed to the Wisconsin Supreme Court, which upheld Justice Smith's ruling and found the Fugitive Slave Act unconstitutional. Arguing that no state court could, under the U.S. Constitution's Supremacy Clause, nullify a federal law, Abelman appealed to the United States Supreme Court.

On March 7, 1859 Chief Justice Roger Taney announced the 9-0 decision of the Court. The edited text follows.

THE ABELMAN COURT

Chief Justice Roger Brooke Taney
Appointed by President Jackson
Served 1836 - 1864

Associate Justice John McLean
Appointed by President Jackson
Served 1829 - 1861

Associate Justice James Wayne
Appointed by President Jackson
Served 1835 - 1867

Associate Justice John Catron
Appointed by President Jackson
Served 1837 - 1865

Associate Justice Peter Daniel
Appointed by President Van Buren
Served 1841 - 1860

Associate Justice Samuel Nelson
Appointed by President Tyler
Served 1845 - 1872

Associate Justice Robert Grier
Appointed by President Polk
Served 1846 - 1870

Associate Justice John Campbell
Appointed by President Pierce
Served 1853 - 1861

Associate Justice Nathan Clifford
Appointed by President Buchanan
Served 1858 - 1881

The unedited text of *Ableman v. Booth* can be found
on page 506, volume 62 of *United States Reports.*

ABLEMAN v. BOOTH
March 7, 1859

CHIEF JUSTICE TANEY: The plaintiff . . . in [this case] is [Stephen V.R. Ableman,] the marshal of the United States for the district of Wisconsin. . . . [T]he following are the facts as they appear in the transcripts before us:

Sherman M. Booth was charged before Winfield Smith, a commissioner duly appointed by the District Court of the United States for the district of Wisconsin, with having, on the 11th day of March, 1854, aided and abetted, at Milwaukee, . . . the escape of a fugitive slave from the deputy marshall, who had him in custody under a warrant issued by the district judge of the United States. . . , under [the Fugitive Slave Act] of September 18, 1850.

. . . . Booth made application . . . to A.D. Smith, one of the justices of the Supreme Court of the State of Wisconsin, for a writ of *habeas corpus* [an order bringing a person before the court], stating that he was restrained of his liberty by Stephen V.R. Ableman, marshal of the United States for that district, under the warrant of commitment hereinbefore mentioned; and alleging that his imprisonment was illegal, because the [Fugitive Slave Act] of September 18, 1850, was unconstitutional and void. . . .

The case was argued before the Supreme Court of the State, and on the 19th of July it pronounced its judgment, affirming [upholding] the decision of the associate justice discharging Booth from imprisonment. . . .

It will be seen . . . that a judge of the Supreme Court of the State of Wisconsin . . . claimed and exercised the right to supervise and annul the proceedings of a commissioner of the United States, and to discharge a prisoner, who had been committed by the commissioner for an offence against the laws of this Government, and that this exercise of power by the judge was afterwards sanctioned and affirmed by the Supreme Court of the State.

. . . . The judges of the Supreme Court of Wisconsin do not distinctly state from what source they suppose they have derived this judicial power. There can be no such thing as judicial authority, unless it is conferred by a Government or sovereignty; and if the judges and courts of Wisconsin possess the jurisdiction they claim, they must derive it either from the United States or the State. It certainly has not been conferred on them by the United States; and it is .equally clear it was not in the power of the State to confer it, even if it had attempted to do so; for no State can authorize one of its judges or courts to exercise judicial power, by *habeas corpus* or otherwise, within the jurisdiction of another and independent Government. . . .

[Q]uestions of this kind must always depend upon the Constitution and laws of the United States, and not of a State. . . .

The language of the Constitution, by which this power is granted, is too plain to admit of doubt or to need comment. It declares that "this Constitution, and the laws of the United States which shall be passed in pursuance thereof, and all treaties made, or which shall be made, under the authority of the United States, shall be the supreme law of the land, and the judges in every State shall be bound thereby, anything in the Constitution or laws of any State to the contrary notwithstanding."

.... These principles of constitutional law are confirmed and illustrated by the clause which confers legislative power upon Congress. That power is specifically given in article 1, section 8, paragraph 18, in the following words:

> "To make all laws which shall be necessary and proper to carry into execution the foregoing powers, and all other powers vested by this Constitution in the Government of the United States, or in any department or officer thereof."

.... The Constitution of the United States, with all the powers conferred by it on the General Government, and surrendered by the States, was the voluntary act of the people of the several States, deliberately done, for their own protection and safety against injustice from one another. . . .

Now, it certainly can be no humiliation to the citizen of a republic to yield a ready obedience to the laws as administered by the constituted authorities. On the contrary, it is among his first and highest duties as a citizen, because free government cannot exist without it. Nor can it be inconsistent with the dignity of a sovereign State to observe faithfully, and in the spirit of sincerity and truth, the compact into which it voluntarily entered when it became a State of this Union. On the contrary, the highest honor of sovereignty is untarnished faith. And certainly no faith could be more deliberately and solemnly pledged than that which every State has plighted to the other States to support the Constitution as it is, in all its provisions, until they shall be altered in the manner which the Constitution itself prescribes. In the emphatic language of the pledge required, it is *to support this Constitution.* And no power is more clearly conferred by

the Constitution and laws of the United States, than the
power of this court to decide, ultimately and finally, all
cases arising under such Constitution and laws. . . .

[I]t can hardly be necessary to point out the errors which
followed their mistaken view of the jurisdiction they
might lawfully exercise; because, if there was any defect
of power in the commissioner, or in his mode of
proceeding, it was for the tribunals of the United States to
revise and correct it, and not for a State court. And as
regards the decision of the District Court, it had exclusive
and final jurisdiction by the laws of the United States;
and neither the regularity of its proceedings nor the
validity of its sentence could be called in question in any
other court, either of a State or the United States, by
habeas corpus or any other process.

. . . . [I]n the judgment of this court, the act of Congress
commonly called the fugitive slave law is, in all of its
provisions, fully authorized by the Constitution of the
United States; that the commissioner had lawful authority
to issue the warrant and commit the party, and that his
proceedings were regular and conformable to the law. . . .

The judgment of the Supreme Court of Wisconsin must
therefore be reversed. . . .

*On June 28, 1864 the United States Congress approved
the repeal of the Fugitive Slave Acts of 1793 and 1850.
The repeal reads in full:* "Be it enacted by the Senate and
the House of Representatives of the United States of
America in Congress assembled, That sections three and
four of an act entitled "An Act respecting fugitives from
justice and persons escaping from the service of their

masters," passed February, seventeen hundred and ninety-three and an act to amend and supplementary to the act entitled "An Act respecting fugitives from justice and persons escaping from the service of their masters," passed February, seventeen hundred and ninety-three," passed September, eighteen hundred and fifty, and the same are hereby repealed."

THE GREAT SLAVERY CASE
Dred Scott v. Sandford

The Constitution is declared to be established for the people. And who are the people? The men and women of the country. We are part of the people; and it is the most unkind - I was going to say it was the most wicked - concession ever made to the slave power from any quarter, to admit that the Constitution does not apply at all to colored people.

Frederick Douglas

Dred Scott, his wife Harriet, and their children, Eliza and Lizzie, were the slaves of Dr. John Emerson, a citizen of Missouri, a slave state. In 1834 Dr. Emerson, a U.S. Army surgeon, was transferred from Missouri to Illinois, a free state. He took the Scotts with him. In 1836 Emerson was transferred from Illinois to Wisconsin, a free territory, and again he took the Scotts with him. In 1838 Dr. Emerson returned with the Scotts to settle in Missouri where in 1843 he died. The Scott family became the property of Emerson's widow, Irene Sanford Emerson, who sold them to her brother John Sanford.

In 1846 Dred Scott began a ten-year legal battle against John Sanford for his freedom. Scott based the case for his freedom on his residence between 1834 and 1838 in a free state and a free territory. Scott sued Sanford (incorrectly spelled Sandford) first in a Missouri Court and then in a Federal Court. Sanford, ignoring Scott's argument that his residence in a free state and free territory had made him free, countered with the argument that Scott, a slave, was neither a citizen of Missouri nor the United States and could not sue in their courts. Both the State and Federal Courts held for Sanford. Dred Scott appealed to the United States Supreme Court.

On March 6, 1857 Chief Justice Roger Taney announced the 7-2 decision of the Court. The edited text follows.

THE DRED SCOTT COURT

Chief Justice Roger Brooke Taney
Appointed by President Jackson
Served 1836 - 1864

Associate Justice John McLean
Appointed by President Jackson
Served 1829 - 1861

Associate Justice James Wayne
Appointed by President Jackson
Served 1835 - 1867

Associate Justice John Catron
Appointed by President Jackson
Served 1837 - 1865

Associate Justice Peter Daniel
Appointed by President Van Buren
Served 1841 - 1860

Associate Justice Samuel Nelson
Appointed by President Tyler
Served 1845 - 1872

Associate Justice Robert Grier
Appointed by President Polk
Served 1846 - 1870

Associate Justice Benjamin Curtis
Appointed by President Fillmore
Served 1851 - 1857

Associate Justice John Campbell
Appointed by President Pierce
Served 1853 - 1861

The unedited text of *Dred Scott v. Sandford* can be found
on page 393, volume 60 of *United States Reports.*

DRED SCOTT v. SANDFORD
March 6, 1857

CHIEF JUSTICE TANEY: The plaintiff [Dred Scott] . . . was, with his wife [Harriet] and children [Eliza and Lizzie], held as slaves by the defendant [John F.A. Sandford], in the State of Missouri; and [Scott] brought this action in the [United States Circuit Court] for that district, to assert the [right] of himself and his family to freedom.

. . . . [Sandford] pleaded . . . that [Scott] was not a citizen of the State of ·Missouri . . . being a negro of African descent, whose ancestors were of pure African blood, and who were brought into this country and sold as slaves.

. . . . The question is simply this: Can a negro, whose ancestors were imported into this country, and sold as slaves, become a member of the political community formed and brought into existence by the Constitution of the United States, and as such become entitled to all the rights, and privileges, and immunities, guarantied by that instrument to the citizen? One of which rights is the privilege of suing in a court of the United States in the cases specified in the Constitution.

. . . . The words "people of the United States" and "citizens" are synonymous. . . . They both describe the political body who, according to our republican institutions, form the sovereignty, and who hold the power and conduct the Government through their representatives. They are what we familiarly call the "sovereign people," and every citizen is one of this people, and a constituent member of this sovereignty. The question before us is, whether the class of persons

described in the plea [the Scott family] . . . compose a
portion of this people, and are constituent members of
this sovereignty? We think they are not, and that they are
not included, and were not intended to be included, under
the word "citizens" in the Constitution, and can therefore
claim none of the rights and privileges which that
instrument provides for and secures to citizens of the
United States. On the contrary, they were at that time
considered as a subordinate and inferior class of beings,
who had been subjugated by the dominant race, and,
whether emancipated or not, yet remained subject to their
authority, and had no rights or privileges but such as
those who held. the power and the Government might
choose to grant them.

It is not the province of the court to decide upon the
justice or injustice, the policy or impolicy, of these laws.
The decision of that question belonged to the political or
law-making power; to those who formed the sovereignty
and framed the Constitution. The duty of the court is, to
interpret the instrument they have framed, with the best
lights we can obtain on the subject, and to administer it as
we find it, according to its true intent and meaning when
it was adopted.

. . . . It is very clear . . . that no State can, by any act or
law of its own, passed since the adoption of the
Constitution, introduce a new member into the political
community created by the Constitution of the United
States. It cannot make him a member of this community
by making him a member of its own. And for the same
reason it cannot introduce any person, or description of
persons, who were not intended to be embraced in this
new political family, which the Constitution brought into
existence, but were intended to be excluded from it.

The question then arises, whether the provisions of the Constitution, in relation to the personal rights and privileges to which the citizen of a State should be entitled, embraced the negro African race, at that time in this country, or who might afterwards be imported, who had then or should afterwards be made free in any State; and to put it in the power of a single State to make him a citizen of the United States, and endue him with the full rights of citizenship in every other State without their consent? Does the Constitution of the United States act upon him whenever he shall be made free under the laws of a State, and raised there to the rank of a citizen, and immediately clothe him with all the privileges of a citizen in every other State, and in its own courts?

The court think the affirmative of these propositions cannot be maintained. And if it cannot, [Scott] could not be a citizen of the State of Missouri, within the meaning of the Constitution of the United States, and, consequently, was not entitled to sue in its courts.

It is true, every person, and every class and description of persons, who were at the time of the adoption of the Constitution recognised as citizens in the several States, became also citizens of this new political body; but none other; it was formed by them, and for them and their posterity, but for no one else. And the personal rights and privileges guarantied to citizens of this new sovereignty were intended to embrace those only who were then members of the several State communities, or who should afterwards by birthright or otherwise become members, according to the provisions of the Constitution and the principles on which it was founded. It was the union of those who were at that time members of distinct and separate political communities into one political family, whose power, for certain specified purposes, was to extend over the whole territory of the United States. And it gave to each citizen rights and privileges outside of his State which he did not before possess, and placed him in every other State upon a perfect equality with its own citizens as to rights of person and rights of property; it made him a citizen of the United States.

It becomes necessary, therefore, to determine who were citizens of the several States when the Constitution was adopted. And in order to do this, we must [go back] to the Governments and institutions of the thirteen colonies, when they separated from Great Britain and formed new sovereignties, and took their places in the family of independent nations. We must inquire who, at that time, were recognised as the people or citizens of a State, whose rights and liberties had been outraged by the English Government; and who declared their independence, and assumed the powers of Government to defend their rights by force of arms.

In the opinion of the court, the legislation and histories of the times, and the language used in the Declaration of Independence, show, that neither the class of persons who had been imported as slaves, nor their descendants, whether they had become free or not, were then acknowledged as a part of the people, nor intended to be included in the general words used in that memorable instrument.

It is difficult at this day to realize the state of public opinion in relation to that unfortunate race, which prevailed in the civilized and enlightened portions of the world at the time of the Declaration of Independence, and when the Constitution of the United States was framed and adopted. But the public history of every European nation displays it in a manner too plain to be mistaken.

They had for more than a century before been regarded as beings of an inferior order, and altogether unfit to associate with the white race, either in social or political relations; and so far inferior, that they had no rights which the white man was bound to respect; and that the negro might justly and lawfully be reduced to slavery for his benefit. He was bought and sold, and treated as an ordinary article of merchandise and traffic, whenever a profit could be made by it. This opinion was at that time fixed and universal in the civilized portion of the white race. It was regarded as an axiom in morals as well as in politics, which no one thought of disputing, or supposed to be open to dispute; and men in every grade and position in society daily and habitually acted upon it in their private pursuits, as well as in matters of public concern, without doubting for a moment the correctness of this opinion.

And in no nation was this opinion more firmly fixed or more uniformly acted upon than by the English Government and English people. They not only seized them on the coast of Africa, and sold them or held them in slavery for their own use; but they took them as ordinary articles of merchandise to every country where they could make a profit on them, and were far more extensively engaged in this commerce than any other nation in the world.

The opinion thus entertained and acted upon in England was naturally impressed upon the colonies they founded on this side of the Atlantic. And, accordingly, a negro of the African race was regarded by them as an article of property, and held, and bought and sold as such, in every one of the thirteen colonies which united in the Declaration of Independence, and afterwards formed the Constitution of the United States. The slaves were more or less numerous in the different colonies, as slave labor was found more or less profitable. But no one seems to have doubted the correctness of the prevailing opinion of the time.

.... The language of the Declaration of Independence is equally conclusive:

It begins by declaring that, "when in the course of human events it becomes necessary for one people to dissolve the political bands which have connected them with another, and to assume among the powers of the earth the separate and equal station to which the laws of nature and nature's God entitle them, a decent respect for the opinions of mankind requires that they should declare the causes which impel them to the separation."

It then proceeds to say: "We hold these truths to be self-evident: that all men are created equal; that they are endowed by their Creator with certain unalienable rights; that among them is life, liberty, and the pursuit of happiness; that to secure these rights, Governments are instituted, deriving their just powers from the consent of the governed."

The general words above quoted would seem to embrace the whole human family, and if they were used in a similar instrument at this day would be so understood. But it is too clear for dispute, that the enslaved African race were not intended to be included, and formed no part of the people who framed and adopted this declaration;

for if the language, as understood in that day, would embrace them, the conduct of the distinguished men who framed the Declaration of Independence would have been utterly and flagrantly inconsistent with the principles they asserted; and instead of the sympathy of mankind, to which they so confidently appealed, they would have deserved and received universal rebuke and reprobation.

Yet the men who framed this declaration were great men - high in literary acquirements - high in their sense of honor, and incapable of asserting principles inconsistent with those on which they were acting. They perfectly understood the meaning of the language they used, and how it would be understood by others; and they knew that it would not in any part of the civilized world be supposed to embrace the negro race, which, by common consent, had been excluded from civilized Governments and the family of nations, and doomed to slavery. They spoke and acted according to the then established doctrines and principles, and in the ordinary language of the day, and no one misunderstood them. The unhappy black race were separated from the white by indelible marks, and laws long before established, and were never thought of or spoken of except as property, and when the claims of the owner or the profit of the trader were supposed to need protection.

This state of public opinion had undergone no change when the Constitution was adopted, as is equally evident from its provisions and language.

The brief preamble sets forth by whom it was formed, for what purposes, and for whose benefit and protection. It declares that it is formed by the *people* of the United States; that is to say, by those who were members of the different political communities in the several States; and its great object is declared to be to secure the blessings of liberty to themselves and their posterity. It speaks in general terms of the *people* of the United States, and of *citizens* of the several States, when it is providing for the exercise of the powers granted or the privileges secured to the citizen. It does not define what description of persons are intended to be included under these terms, or who shall be regarded as a citizen and one of the people. It uses them as terms so well understood, that no further description or definition was necessary.

But there are two clauses in the Constitution which point directly and specifically to the negro race as a separate class of persons, and show clearly that they were not regarded as a portion of the people or citizens of the Government then formed.

One of these clauses reserves to each of the thirteen States the right to import slaves until the year 1808, if it thinks proper. And the importation which it thus sanctions was unquestionably of persons of the race of which we are speaking, as the traffic in slaves in the United States had always been confined to them. And by the other provision the States pledge themselves to each other to maintain the right of property of the master, by delivering up to him any slave who may have escaped from his service, and be found within their respective territories. By the first above-mentioned clause, therefore, the right to purchase and hold this property is directly sanctioned and authorized for twenty years by the people who framed the Constitution. And by the second, they pledge themselves to maintain and uphold the right of the master in the manner specified, as long as the Government they then formed should endure. And these two provisions show, conclusively, that neither the description of persons therein referred to, nor their descendants, were embraced in any of the other provisions of the Constitution; for certainly these two clauses were not intended to confer on them or their posterity the blessings of liberty, or any of the personal rights so carefully provided for the citizen.

No one of that race had ever migrated to the United States voluntarily; all of them had been brought here as articles of merchandise.   The number that had been emancipated at that time were but few in comparison with those held in slavery; and they were identified in the public mind with the race to which they belonged, and regarded as a part of the slave population rather than the free. It is obvious that they were not even in the minds of the framers of the Constitution when they were conferring special rights and privileges upon the citizens of a State in every other part of the Union.

Indeed, when we look to the condition of this race in the several States at the time, it is impossible to believe that these rights and privileges were intended to be extended to them.

It is very true, that in the portion of the Union where the labor of the negro race was found to be unsuited to the climate and unprofitable to the master, but few slaves were held at the time of the Declaration of Independence; and when the Constitution was adopted, it had entirely worn out in one of them, and measures had been taken for its gradual abolition in several others.   But this change had not been produced by any change of opinion in relation to this race; but because it was discovered, from experience, that slave labor was unsuited to the climate and productions of these States: for some of the States, where it had ceased or nearly ceased to exist, were actively engaged in the slave trade, procuring cargoes on the coast of Africa, and transporting them for sale to those parts of the Union where their labor was found to be profitable, and suited to the climate and productions. And this traffic was openly carried on, and fortunes accumulated by it, without reproach from the people of the States where they resided. And it can hardly be supposed that, in the States where it was then countenanced in its worst form - that is, in the seizure and transportation - the people could have regarded those who were emancipated as entitled to equal rights with themselves.

. . . . The legislation of [several] States [Maryland, Connecticut, New Hampshire, Rhode Island, Massachusetts] . . . shows, in a manner not to be mistaken, the inferior and subject condition of that race at the time the Constitution was adopted, and long afterwards, throughout the thirteen States by which that instrument was framed; and it is hardly consistent with the respect due to these States, to suppose that they regarded at that time, as fellow-citizens and members of the sovereignty, a class of beings whom they had thus stigmatized; whom, as we are bound, out of respect to the State sovereignties, to assume they had deemed it just and necessary thus to stigmatize, and upon whom they had impressed such deep and enduring marks of inferiority and degradation; or, that when they met in convention to form the Constitution, they looked upon them as a portion of their constituents, or designed to include them in the provisions so carefully inserted for the security and protection of the liberties and rights of their citizens. It cannot be supposed that they intended to secure to them rights, and privileges, and rank, in the new political body throughout the Union, which every one of them denied within the limits of its own dominion. More especially, it cannot be believed that the large slaveholding States regarded them as included in the word citizens, or would have consented to a Constitution which might compel them to receive them in that character from another State. For if they were so received, and entitled to the privileges and immunities of citizens, it would exempt them from the operation of the special laws and from the police regulations which they considered to be necessary for their own safety. It would give to persons of the negro race, who were recognised as citizens in any one State of the Union, the right to enter every other State whenever they pleased, singly or in companies, without pass or passport, and without obstruction, to sojourn there as long as they pleased, to go where they pleased at every hour of the day or night without molestation, unless they committed some violation of law for which a white man would be punished; and it would give them the full liberty of speech in public and in private upon all subjects upon which its own citizens might speak; to hold public meetings upon political affairs, and to keep and carry arms wherever they went. And all of this would be done in the face of the subject race of the same color, both free and slaves, and inevitably producing discontent and insubordination among them, and endangering the peace and safety of the State.

It is impossible, it would seem, to believe that the great men of the slaveholding States, who took so large a share in framing the Constitution of the United States, and exercised so much influence in procuring its adoption, could have been so forgetful or regardless of their own safety and the safety of those who trusted and confided in them.

. . . . A clause similar to the one in the Constitution, in relation to the rights and immunities of citizens of one State in the other States, was contained in the Articles of Confederation. But there is a difference of language, which is worthy of note. The provision in the Articles of Confederation was, "that the *free inhabitants* of each of the States, paupers, vagabonds, and fugitives from justice, excepted, should be entitled to all the privileges and immunities of free citizens in the several States."

It will be observed, that under this Confederation, each State had the right to decide for itself, and in its own tribunals, whom it would acknowledge as a free inhabitant of another State. The term *free inhabitant*, in the generality of its terms, would certainly include one of the African race who had been [freed from slavery]. But no example, we think, can be found of his admission to all the privileges of citizenship in any State of the Union after these Articles were formed, and while they continued in force. And, notwithstanding the generality of the words "free inhabitants," it is very clear that, according to their accepted meaning in that day, they did not include the African race, whether free or not: for the fifth section of the ninth article provides that Congress should have the power "to agree upon the number of land forces to be raised, and to make requisitions from each State for its quota in proportion to the number of *white* inhabitants in such State, which requisition should be binding."

Words could hardly have been used which more strongly mark the line of distinction between the citizen and the subject; the free and the subjugated races. The latter were not even counted when the inhabitants of a State were to be embodied in proportion to its numbers for the general defence. And it cannot for a moment be supposed, that a class of persons thus separated and rejected from those who formed the sovereignty of the States, were yet intended to be included under the words "free inhabitants," in the preceding article, to whom privileges and immunities were so carefully secured in every State.

But although this clause of the Articles of Confederation is the same in principle with that inserted in the Constitution, yet the comprehensive word *inhabitant*, which might be construed [interpreted] to include an emancipated slave, is omitted; and the privilege is confined to *citizens* of the State. And this alteration in words would hardly have been made, unless a different meaning was intended to be conveyed, or a possible doubt removed. The just and fair inference is, that as this privilege was about to be placed under the protection of the General Government, and the words expounded by its tribunals, and all power in relation to it taken from the State and its courts, it was deemed prudent to describe with precision and caution the persons to whom this high privilege was given - and the word *citizen* was on that account substituted for the words *free inhabitant.* The word citizen excluded, and no doubt intended to exclude, foreigners who had not become citizens of some one of the States when the Constitution was adopted; and also every description of persons who were not fully recognised as citizens in the several States. This, upon any fair construction of the instruments to which we have referred, was evidently the object and purpose of this change of words.

To all this mass of proof we have still to add, that Congress has repeatedly legislated upon the same construction of the Constitution that we have given. Three laws, two of which were passed almost immediately after the Government went into operation, will be abundantly sufficient to show this. The two first are particularly worthy of notice, because many of the men who assisted in framing the Constitution, and took an active part in procuring its adoption, were then in the halls of legislation, and certainly understood what they meant when they used the words "people of the United States" and "citizen" in that well-considered instrument.

The first of these acts is the naturalization law, which was passed at the second session of the first Congress, March 26, 1790, and confines the right of becoming citizens "*to aliens being free white persons.*"

Now, the Constitution does not limit the power of Congress in this respect to white persons. And they may, if they think proper, authorize the naturalization of any one, of any color, who was born under allegiance to another Government. But the language of the law above quoted, shows that citizenship at that time was perfectly understood to be confined to the white race; and that they alone constituted the sovereignty in the Government.

. . . . Another of the early laws of which we have spoken, is the first militia law, which was passed in 1792, at the first session of the second Congress. The language of this law is equally plain and significant with the one just mentioned. It directs that every "free able-bodied white male citizen" shall be enrolled in the militia. The word *white* is evidently used to exclude the African race, and the word "citizen" to exclude unnaturalized foreigners;

the latter forming no part of the sovereignty, owing it no allegiance, and therefore under no obligation to defend it. The African race, however, born in the country, did owe allegiance to the Government, whether they were slave or free; but it is repudiated, and rejected from the duties and obligations of citizenship in marked language.

The third act to which we have alluded is even still more decisive; it was passed as late as 1813, and it provides: "That from and after the termination of the war in which the United States are now engaged with Great Britain, it shall not be lawful to employ, on board of any public or private vessels of the United States, any person or persons except citizens of the United States, *or* persons of color, natives of the United States.

Here the line of distinction is drawn in express words. Persons of color, in the judgment of Congress, were not included in the word citizens, and they are described as another and different class of persons, and authorized to be employed, if born in the United States.

And even as late as 1820, in the charter to the city of Washington, the corporation is authorized "to restrain and prohibit the nightly and other disorderly meetings of slaves, free negroes, and mulattoes," thus associating them together in its legislation; and after prescribing the punishment that may be inflicted on the slaves, proceeds in the following words: "And to punish such free negroes and mulattoes by penalties not exceeding twenty dollars for any one offence; and in case of the inability of any such free negro or mulatto to pay any such penalty and cost thereon, to cause him or her to be confined to labor for any time not exceeding six calendar months." And in a subsequent part of the same section, the act authorizes the corporation "to prescribe the terms and conditions upon which free negroes and mulattoes may reside in the city."

This law, like the laws of the States, shows that this class of persons were governed by special legislation directed expressly to them, and always connected with provisions for the government of slaves, and not with those for the government of free white citizens. And, after such an uniform course of legislation as we have stated, by the colonies, by the States, and by Congress, running through a period of more than a century, it would seem that to call persons thus marked and stigmatized, "citizens" of the United States, "fellow-citizens," a constituent part of the sovereignty, would be an abuse of terms, and not calculated to exalt the character of an American citizen in the eyes of other nations.

. . . . The only two provisions [in the U.S. Constitution] which point to them and include them, treat them as property, and make it the duty of the Government to protect it; no other power, in relation to this race, is to be found in the Constitution; and as it is a Government of special, delegated powers, no authority beyond these two provisions can be constitutionally exercised. The Government of the United States had no right to interfere for any other purpose but that of protecting the rights of the owner, leaving it altogether with the several States to deal with this race, whether emancipated or not, as each State may think justice, humanity, and the interests and safety of society, require. The States evidently intended to reserve this power exclusively to themselves.

No one, we presume, supposes that any change in public opinion or feeling, in relation to this unfortunate race, in the civilized nations of Europe or in this country, should induce the court to give to the words of the Constitution a more liberal construction in their favor than they were intended to bear when the instrument was framed and adopted. Such an argument would be altogether inadmissible in any tribunal called on to interpret it. If any of its provisions are deemed unjust, there is a mode prescribed in the instrument itself by which it may be amended; but while it remains unaltered, it must be construed now as it was understood at the time of its adoption. It is not only the same in words, but the same in meaning, and delegates the same powers to the Government, and reserves and secures the same rights and privileges to the citizen; and as long as it continues to exist in its present form, it speaks not only in the same words, but with the same meaning and intent with which it spoke when it came from the hands of its framers, and was voted on and adopted by the people of the United States. Any other rule of construction would abrogate [annul] the judicial character of this court, and make it the mere reflex of the popular opinion or passion of the day. This court was not created by the Constitution for such purposes. Higher and graver trusts have been confided to it, and it must not falter in the path of duty.

What the construction was at that time, we think can hardly admit of doubt. We have the language of the Declaration of Independence and of the Articles of Confederation, in addition to the plain words of the Constitution itself; we have the legislation of the different States, before, about the time, and since, the Constitution was adopted; we have the legislation of Congress, from the time of its adoption to a recent period; and we have the constant and uniform action of the Executive Department, all concurring together, and

leading to the same result. And if anything in relation to
the construction of the Constitution can be regarded as
settled, it is that which we now give to the word "citizen"
and the word "people."

And upon a full and careful consideration of the subject,
the court is of opinion, that . . . Dred Scott was not a
citizen of Missouri within the meaning of the
Constitution of the United States, and not entitled as such
to sue in its courts. . . .

[F]or he admits that he and his wife were born slaves, but
endeavors to make out his [right] to freedom and
citizenship by showing that they were taken by their
owner to [Illinois and Wisconsin, then a part of the
Louisiana Territory] where slavery could not by law exist,
and that they thereby became free, and upon their return
to Missouri became citizens of that State.

Now, if the removal of which he speaks did not give them
their freedom, then by his own admission he is still a
slave; and whatever opinions may be entertained in favor
of the citizenship of a free person of the African race, no
one supposes that a slave is a citizen of the State or of the
United States. If, therefore, the acts done by his owner
did not make them free persons, he is still a slave, and
certainly incapable of suing in the character of a citizen.

. . . . In considering this part of the controversy, two
questions arise: 1. Was he, together with his family, free
in Missouri by reason of the stay in the territory of the
United States hereinbefore mentioned? And 2. If they
were not, is Scott himself free by reason of his removal to
Rock Island, in the State of Illinois, as stated in the above
admissions?

. . . . [The Missouri Compromise, the] act of Congress, upon which [Scott] relies, declares that slavery and involuntary servitude, except as a punishment for crime, shall be forever prohibited in all that part of the territory ceded by France, under the name of Louisiana, which lies north of thirty-six degrees thirty minutes north latitude, and not included within the limits of Missouri. . . .

Now, as we have already said in an earlier part of this opinion . . . the right of property in a slave is distinctly and expressly affirmed in the Constitution. The right to traffic in it, like an ordinary article of merchandise and property, was guarantied to the citizens of the United States, in every State that might desire it, for twenty years. And the Government in express terms is pledged to protect it in all future time, if the slave escapes from his owner. This is done in plain words - too plain to be misunderstood. And no word can be found in the Constitution which gives Congress a greater power over slave property, or which entitles property of that kind to less protection than property of any other description. The only power conferred is the power coupled with the duty of guarding and protecting the owner in his rights.

Upon these considerations, it is the opinion of the court that the [Missouri Compromise] which prohibited a citizen from holding and owning property of this kind in the territory of the United States north of the line therein mentioned, is not warranted by the Constitution, and is therefore void; and that neither Dred Scott himself, nor any of his family, were made free by being carried into this territory; even if they had been carried there by the owner, with the intention of becoming a permanent resident.

.... Upon the whole, therefore, it is the judgment of this court, that it appears by the record before us that [Dred Scott] is not a citizen of Missouri, in the sense in which that word is used in the Constitution; and that the Circuit Court of the United States, for that reason, had no jurisdiction in the case, and could give no judgment in it. Its judgment for [Sandford] must, consequently, be reversed, and a mandate [order to the lower Court] issued, directing the suit to be dismissed for want of jurisdiction.

On May 26, 1857 Dred Scott, purchased from slaveholder John Sanford by abolitionist Taylor Blow, was finally freed from slavery. Scott died in 1858.

The Thirteenth Amendment, which prohibits slavery in the United States, called by many the "Dred Scott Amendment," was enacted in 1865. The Thirteenth Amendment reads in full: Neither slavery nor involuntary servitude, except as punishment for crime whereof the party shall have been duly convicted, shall exist within the United States, or any place subject to their jurisdiction.

The Fourteenth Amendment's Citizenship Clause, enacted in 1868, made all former slaves citizens of both the United States and the States of their residence.

THE SEGREGATION CASES

The Slaughterhouse Cases

No state shall make or enforce any law which shall abridge the privileges or immunities of citizens of the United States.

The Privileges or Immunities Clause
The Fourteenth Amendment

The Thirteenth, Fourteenth, and Fifteenth Amendments were ratified by the states on December 6, 1865, July 9, 1868, and March 30, 1870, respectively. They are known collectively as the Reconstruction Amendments and were written specifically to protect the legal rights of former slaves. The first case to reach the Supreme Court was not filed by former slaves, but by angry butchers.

On March 8, 1869 the Louisiana Legislature, in an action purportedly to protect the health of the people of New Orleans, enacted the Slaughterhouse Law, which created a twenty-five year business monopoly for the Crescent City Slaughterhouse Company in the slaughtering of animals in and around the city of New Orleans. The Butchers Benevolent Association of New Orleans was a group of independent butchers whose members were forbidden under the Slaughterhouse Law to practice their trade except in the employ of, or by paying a fee to, the Slaughterhouse Company. They filed a civil rights suit claiming that the Slaughterhouse Law was an unconstitutional violation of their civil rights under the Involuntary Servitude Clause of the Thirteenth Amendment and the Privileges or Immunities, Equal Protection, and Due Process Clauses of the Fourteenth Amendment. The Louisiana Supreme Court decided in favor of the Slaughterhouse Company and the Butchers Benevolent Association appealed to the United States Supreme Court.

On April 14, 1873 Justice Samuel Miller announced the 5-4 decision of the Court. The edited text follows.

THE SLAUGHTERHOUSE COURT

Chief Justice Salmon P. Chase
Appointed by President Lincoln
Served 1864 - 1873

Associate Justice Nathan Clifford
Appointed by President Buchanan
Served 1858 - 1881

Associate Justice Noah Swayne
Appointed by President Lincoln
Served 1862 - 1881

Associate Justice Samuel Miller
Appointed by President Lincoln
Served 1862 - 1890

Associate Justice David Davis
Appointed by President Lincoln
Served 1862 - 1877

Associate Justice Stephen Field
Appointed by President Lincoln
Served 1863 - 1897

Associate Justice William Strong
Appointed by President Grant
Served 1870 - 1880

Associate Justice Joseph Bradley
Appointed by President Grant
Served 1870 - 1892

Associate Justice Ward Hunt
Appointed by President Grant
Served 1873 - 1882

The unedited text of *The Slaughterhouse Cases* can be found on page 36, volume 83 of *United States Reports*.

THE SLAUGHTERHOUSE CASES
April 14, 1873

JUSTICE MILLER: These cases are brought here [from] the Supreme Court of the State of Louisiana. They arise out of the efforts of the butchers of New Orleans to resist the [Crescent City Slaughterhouse Company] in the exercise of certain powers conferred by the charter which created it, and which was granted by the legislature of that State.

. . . . The records show that the plaintiffs [Butchers' Benevolent Association of New Orleans] relied upon, and asserted throughout the entire course of the litigation in the State courts, that the grant of privileges in the charter of defendant [the slaughterhouse], which they were contesting, was a violation of the most important provisions of the thirteenth and fourteenth articles of amendment of the Constitution of the United States. The jurisdiction and the duty of this court to review the judgment of the State court on those questions is clear and is imperative.

The statute thus assailed as unconstitutional was passed March 8th, 1869, and is entitled "An act to protect the health of the city of New Orleans, to locate the stock-landings and slaughterhouses, and to incorporate the Crescent City Livestock Landing and Slaughterhouse Company."

. . . . This statute is denounced not only as creating a monopoly and conferring odious and exclusive privileges upon a small number of persons at the expense of the great body of the community of New Orleans, but it is asserted that it deprives a large and meritorious class of citizens - the whole of the butchers of the city - of the right

to exercise their trade, the business to which they have
been trained and on which they depend for the support of
themselves and their families; and that the unrestricted
exercise of the business of butchering is necessary to the
daily subsistence of the population of the city.

. . . . The [Butchers' Benevolent Association] allege[s] that
the statute is a violation of the Constitution of the United
States in these several particulars:

> That it creates an involuntary servitude forbid-
> den by the thirteenth article of amendment;

> That it abridges the privileges and immunities of
> citizens of the United States;

> That it denies to the [Butchers' Benevolent
> Association] the equal protection of the laws;
> and,

> That it deprives them of their property without
> due process of law; contrary to the provisions of
> the first section of the fourteenth article of
> amendment.

This court is thus called upon for the first time to give
construction to these articles.

We do not conceal from ourselves the great responsibility
which this duty devolves upon us. No questions so far-
reaching and pervading in their consequences, so pro-
foundly interesting to the people of this country, and so
important in their bearing upon the relations of the United States, and to the several States to each other and to the

citizens of the States and of the United States, have been before this court during the official life of any of its present members. We have given every opportunity for a full hearing at the bar; we have discussed it freely and compared views among ourselves; we have taken ample time for careful deliberation, and we now propose to announce the judgments which we have formed in the construction of those articles, so far as we have found them necessary to the decision of the cases before us, and beyond that we have neither the inclination nor the right to go.

Twelve articles of amendment were added to the Federal Constitution soon after the original organization of the government under it in 1789. Of these all but the last were adopted so soon afterwards as to justify the statement that they were practically contemporaneous with the adoption of the original; and the twelfth, adopted in eighteen hundred and three, was so nearly so as to have become, like all the others, historical and of another age. But within the last eight years three other articles of amendment of vast importance have been added by the voice of the people to that now venerable instrument.

The most cursory glance at these articles discloses a unity of purpose, when taken in connection with the history of the times, which cannot fail to have an important bearing on any question of doubt concerning their true meaning. Nor can such doubts, when any reasonably exist, be safely and rationally solved without a reference to that history; for in it is found the occasion and the necessity for recurring again to the great source of power in this country, the people of the States, for additional guarantees of human rights; additional powers to the Federal government; additional restraints upon those of the States. Fortunately that history is fresh within the memory of us all, and its leading features, as they bear upon the matter before us, free from doubt.

The institution of African slavery, as it existed in about half the States of the Union, and the contests pervading the public mind for many years, between those who desired its curtailment and ultimate extinction and those who desired additional safeguards for its security and perpetuation, culminated in the effort, on the part of most of the States in which slavery existed, to separate from the Federal government, and to resist its authority. This constituted the war of the rebellion, and whatever auxiliary causes may have contributed to bring about this war, undoubtedly the overshadowing and efficient cause was African slavery.

In that struggle slavery, as a legalized social relation, perished. It perished as a necessity of the bitterness and force of the conflict. When the armies of freedom found themselves upon the soil of slavery they could do nothing less than free the poor victims whose enforced servitude was the foundation of the quarrel. And when hard pressed in the contest these men (for they proved themselves men in that terrible crisis) offered their services and were accepted by thousands to aid in suppressing the unlawful rebellion, slavery was at an end wherever the Federal government succeeded in that purpose. The proclamation of President Lincoln expressed an accomplished fact as to a large portion of the insurrectionary districts, when he declared slavery abolished in them all. But the war being over, those who had succeeded in reestablishing the authority of the Federal government were not content to permit this great act of emancipation to rest on the actual results of the contest or the proclamation of the Ex-

ecutive, both of which might have been questioned in after times, and they determined to place this main and most
valuable result in the Constitution of the restored Union
as one of its fundamental articles. Hence the thirteenth
article of amendment of that instrument. Its two short
sections seem hardly to admit of construction, so vigorous
is their expression and so appropriate to the purpose we
have indicated.

> "1. Neither slavery nor involuntary servitude, ex-
> cept as a punishment for crime, whereof the par-
> ty shall have been duly convicted, shall exist
> within the United States or any place subject to
> their jurisdiction.

> "2. Congress shall have the power to enforce this
> article by appropriate legislation."

To withdraw the mind from the contemplation of this
grand yet simple declaration of the personal freedom of
all the human race within the jurisdiction of this government - a declaration designed to establish the freedom of
four millions of slaves - and with a microscopic search en-
deavor to find in it a reference to servitudes, which may
have been attached to property in certain localities, requires an effort, to say the least of it.

That a personal servitude was meant is proved by the use
of the word "involuntary," which can only apply to human
beings. The exception of servitude as a punishment for
crime gives an idea of the class of servitude that is meant.
The word servitude is of larger meaning than slavery, as
the latter is popularly understood in this country, and the
obvious purpose was to forbid all shades and conditions of
African slavery. It was very well understood that in the

form of apprenticeship for long terms, as it had been practiced in the West India Islands, on the abolition of slavery by the English government, or by reducing the slaves to the condition of serfs attached to the plantation, the purpose of the article might have been evaded, if only the word slavery had been used. The case of the apprentice slave, held under a law of Maryland, liberated by Chief Justice Chase, on a writ of habeas corpus [an order bringing a person before the court] under this article, illustrates this course of observation. And it is all that we deem necessary to say on the application of that article to the statute of Louisiana, now under consideration.

The process of restoring to their proper relations with the Federal government and with the other States those which had sided with the rebellion, undertaken under the proclamation of President [Andrew] Johnson in 1865, and before the assembling of Congress, developed the fact that, notwithstanding the formal recognition by those States of the abolition of slavery, the condition of the slave race would, without further protection of the Federal government, be almost as bad as it was before. Among the first acts of legislation adopted by several of the States in the legislative bodies which claimed to be in their normal relations with the Federal government, were laws which imposed upon the colored race onerous disabilities and burdens, and curtailed their rights in the pursuit of life, liberty, and property to such an extent that their freedom was of little value, while they had lost the protection which they had received from their former owners from motives both of interest and humanity.

They were in some States forbidden to appear in the towns in any other character than menial servants. They were required to reside on and cultivate the soil without

the right to purchase or own it. They were excluded from
many occupations of gain, and were not permitted to give
testimony in the courts in any case where a white man
was a party. It was said that their lives were at the mercy
of bad men, either because the laws for their protection
were insufficient or were not enforced.

These circumstances, whatever of falsehood or misconcep-
tion may have been mingled with their presentation,
forced upon the statesmen who had conducted the Federal
government in safety through the crisis of the rebellion,
and who supposed that by the thirteenth article of amendment they had secured the result of their labors, the conviction that something more was necessary in the way of
constitutional protection to the unfortunate race who had
suffered so much. They accordingly passed through Congress the proposition for the fourteenth amendment, and
they declined to treat as restored to their full participation in the government of the Union the States which had
been in insurrection, until they ratified that article by a
formal vote of their legislative bodies.

Before we proceed to examine more critically the provisions of this amendment, on which the [Butchers' Benevolent Association] rel[ies], let us complete and dismiss the
history of the recent amendments, as that history relates
to the general purpose which pervades them all. A few
years' experience satisfied the thoughtful men who had
been the authors of the other two amendments that, notwithstanding the restraints of those articles on the States,
and the laws passed under the additional powers granted
to Congress, these were inadequate for the protection of
life, liberty, and property, without which freedom to the
slave was no boon. They were in all those States denied
the right of suffrage. The laws were administered by the

white man alone. It was urged that a race of men distinctively marked as was the negro, living in the midst of another and dominant race, could never be fully secured in their person and their property without the right of suffrage.

Hence the fifteenth amendment, which declares that "the right of a citizen of the United States to vote shall not be denied or abridged by any State on account of race, color, or previous condition of servitude." The negro having, by the fourteenth amendment, been declared to be a citizen of the United States, is thus made a voter in every State of the Union.

We repeat, then, in the light of this recapitulation of events, almost too recent to be called history, but which are familiar to us all; and on the most casual examination of the language of these amendments, no one can fail to be impressed with the one pervading purpose found in them all, lying at the foundation of each, and without which none of them would have been even suggested; we mean the freedom of the slave race, the security and firm establishment of that freedom, and the protection of the newly-made freeman and citizen from the oppressions of those who had formerly exercised unlimited dominion over him. It is true that only the fifteenth amendment, in terms, mentions the negro by speaking of his color and his slavery. But it is just as true that each of the other articles was addressed to the grievances of that race, and designed to remedy them as the fifteenth.

We do not say that no one else but the negro can share in this protection. Both the language and spirit of these articles are to have their fair and just weight in any question of construction. Undoubtedly while negro slavery alone was in the mind of the Congress which proposed the thirteenth article, it forbids any other kind of slavery, now or hereafter. If Mexican peonage or the Chinese coolie labor system shall develop slavery of the Mexican or Chinese race within our territory, this amendment may safely be trusted to make it void. And so if other rights are assailed by the States which properly and necessarily fall within the protection of these articles, that protection will apply, though the party interested may not be of African descent. But what we do say, and what we wish to be understood is, that in any fair and just construction of any section or phrase of these amendments, it is necessary to look to the purpose which we have said was the pervading spirit of them all, the evil which they were designed to remedy, and the process of continued addition to the Constitution, until that purpose was supposed to be accomplished, as far as constitutional law can accomplish it.

The first section of the fourteenth article, to which our attention is more specially invited, opens with a definition of citizenship - not only citizenship of the United States, but citizenship of the States. No such definition was previously found in the Constitution, nor had any attempt been made to define it by act of Congress. It had been the occasion of much discussion in the courts, by the executive departments, and in the public journals. It had been said by eminent judges that no man was a citizen of the United States, except as he was a citizen of one of the States composing the Union. Those, therefore, who had been born and resided always in the District of Columbia or in the Territories, though within the United States, were not citizens. Whether this proposition was sound or not had never been judicially decided. But it had been held by this court, in the celebrated Dred Scott case, only a few years before the outbreak of the civil war, that a

man of African descent, whether a slave or not, was not
and could not be a citizen of a State or of the United
States. This decision, while it met the condemnation of
some of the ablest statesmen and constitutional lawyers of
the country, had never been overruled; and if it was to be
accepted as a constitutional limitation of the right of citizenship, then all the negro race who had recently been
made freemen, were still, not only not citizens, but were
incapable of becoming so by anything short of an amendment to the Constitution.

To remove this difficulty primarily, and to establish a
clear and comprehensive definition of citizenship which
should declare what should constitute citizenship of the
United States, and also citizenship of a State, the first
clause of the first section was framed.

> "All persons born or naturalized in the United
> States, and subject to the jurisdiction thereof, are
> citizens of the United States and of the State
> wherein they reside."

The first observation we have to make on this clause is,
that it puts at rest both the questions which we stated to
have been the subject of differences of opinion. It declares that persons may be citizens of the United States
without regard to their citizenship of a particular State,
and it overturns the Dred Scott decision by making *all
persons* born within the United States and subject to its
jurisdiction citizens of the United States. That its main
purpose was to establish the citizenship of the negro can
admit of no doubt. The phrase, "subject to its jurisdiction" was intended to exclude from its operation children
of ministers, consuls, and citizens or subjects of foreign
States born within the United States.

The next observation is more important in view of the arguments of counsel in the present case. It is, that the distinction between citizenship of the United States and citizenship of a State is clearly recognized and established. Not only may a man be a citizen of the United States without being a citizen of a State, but an important element is necessary to convert the former into the latter. He must reside within the State to make him a citizen of it, but it is only necessary that he should be born or naturalized in the United States to be a citizen of the Union.

It is quite clear, then, that there is a citizenship of the United States, and a citizenship of a State, which are distinct from each other, and which depend upon different characteristics or circumstances in the individual.

We think this distinction and its explicit recognition in this amendment of great weight in this argument, because the next paragraph of this same section, which is the one mainly relied on by the [Butchers' Benevolent Association], speaks only of privileges and immunities of citizens of the United States, and does not speak of those of citizens of the several States. The argument, however, in favor of the [Butchers' Benevolent Association] rests wholly on the assumption that the citizenship is the same, and the privileges and immunities guaranteed by the clause are the same.

The language is, "No State shall make or enforce any law which shall abridge the privileges or immunities of citizens of *the United States.*" It is a little remarkable, if this clause was intended as a protection to the citizen of a State against the legislative power of his own State, that the word citizen of the State should be left out when it is so carefully used, and used in contradistinction to citizens of the United States, in the very sentence which precedes it. It is too clear for argument that the change in phraseology was adopted understandingly and with a purpose.

Of the privileges and immunities of the citizen of the United States, and of the privileges and immunities of the citizen of the State, and what they respectively are, we will presently consider; but we wish to state here that it is only the former which are placed by this clause under the protection of the Federal Constitution, and that the latter, whatever they may be, are not intended to have any additional protection by this paragraph of the amendment.

If, then, there is a difference between the privileges and immunities belonging to a citizen of the United States as such, and those belonging to the citizen of the State as such, the latter must rest for their security and protection where they have heretofore rested; for they are not embraced by this paragraph of the amendment.

The first occurrence of the words "privileges and immunities" in our constitutional history, is to be found in the fourth of the articles of the old Confederation.

It declares "that the better to secure and perpetuate mutual friendship and intercourse among the people of the different States in this Union, the free inhabitants of each of these States, paupers, vagabonds, and fugitives from justice excepted, shall be entitled to all the privileges and immunities of free citizens in the several States; and the people of each State shall have free ingress and regress to and from any other State, and shall enjoy therein all the privileges of trade and commerce, subject to the same duties, impositions, and restrictions as the inhabitants thereof respectively."

In the Constitution of the United States, which superseded the Articles of Confederation, the corresponding provision is found in section two of the fourth article, in the following words: "The citizens of each State shall be entitled to all the privileges and immunities of citizens of the several States."

There can be but little question that the purpose of both these provisions is the same, and that the privileges and immunities intended are the same in each. In the article of the Confederation we have some of these specifically mentioned, and enough perhaps to give some general idea of the class of civil rights meant by the phrase.

Fortunately we are not without judicial construction of this clause of the Constitution. The first and the leading case on the subject is that of *Corfield v. Coryell*, decided by Justice Washington in the Circuit Court for the District of Pennsylvania in 1823.

"The inquiry," he says, "is, what are the privileges and immunities of citizens of the several States? We feel no hesitation in confining these expressions to those privileges and immunities which are *fundamental*, which belong of right to the citizens of all free governments, and which have at all times been enjoyed by citizens of the several States which compose this Union, from the time of their becoming free, independent, and sovereign. What these fundamental principles are, it would be more tedious than difficult to enumerate. They may all, however, be comprehended under the following general heads: protection by the government, with the right to acquire and possess property of every kind, and to pursue and obtain happiness and safety, subject, nevertheless, to such restraints as the government may prescribe for the general good of the whole."

This definition of the privileges and immunities of citizens of the States is adopted in the main by this court in the recent case of *Ward v. Maryland,* while it declines to undertake an authoritative definition beyond what was necessary to that decision. The description, when taken to include others not named, but which are of the same general character, embraces nearly every civil right for the establishment and protection of which organized government is instituted. They are, in the language of Judge Washington, those rights which are fundamental. Throughout his opinion, they are spoken of as rights belonging to the individual as a citizen of a State. They are so spoken of in the constitutional provision which he was construing [interpreting]. And they have always been held to be the class of rights which the State governments were created to establish and secure.

In the case of *Paul v. Virginia,* the court, in expounding this clause of the Constitution, says that "the privileges and immunities secured to citizens of each State in the several States, by the provision in question, are those privileges and immunities which are common to the citizens in the latter States under their constitution and laws by virtue of their being citizens."

The constitutional provision there alluded to did not create those rights, which it called privileges and immunities of citizens of the States. It threw around them in that clause no security for the citizen of the State in which they were claimed or exercised. Nor did it profess to control the power of the State governments over the rights of its own citizens.

Its sole purpose was to declare to the several States, that whatever those rights, as you grant or establish them to your own citizens, or as you limit or qualify, or impose restrictions on their exercise, the same, neither more nor less, shall be the measure of the rights of citizens of other States within your jurisdiction.

It would be the vainest show of learning to attempt to prove by citations of authority, that up to the adoption of the recent amendments, no claim or pretence was set up that those rights depended on the Federal government for their existence or protection, beyond the very few express limitations which the Federal Constitution imposed upon the States - such, for instance, as the prohibition against ex post facto [after the fact] laws, bills of attainder [acts of the legislature calling for capital punishment for a high crime], and laws impairing the obligation of contracts. But with the exception of these and a few other restrictions, the entire domain of the privileges and immunities of citizens of the States, as above defined, lay within the constitutional and legislative power of the States, and without that of the Federal government. Was it the purpose of the fourteenth amendment, by the simple declaration that no State should make or enforce any law which shall abridge the privileges and immunities of *citizens of the United States*, to transfer the security and protection of all the civil rights which we have mentioned, from the States to the Federal government? And where it is declared that Congress shall have the power to enforce that article, was it intended to bring within the power of Congress the entire domain of civil rights heretofore belonging exclusively to the States?

All this and more must follow, if the proposition of the [Butchers' Benevolent Association] be sound. For not only are these rights subject to the control of Congress whenever in its discretion any of them are supposed to be abridged by State legislation, but that body may also pass laws in advance, limiting and restricting the exercise of legislative power by the States, in their most ordinary and usual functions, as in its judgment it may think proper on all such subjects. And still further, such a construction followed by the reversal of the judgments of the Supreme Court of Louisiana in these cases, would constitute this court a perpetual censor upon all legislation of the States, on the civil rights of their own citizens, with authority to nullify such as it did not approve as consistent with those rights, as they existed at the time of the adoption of this amendment. The argument we admit is not always the most conclusive which is drawn from the consequences urged against the adoption of a particular construction of an instrument. But when, as in the case before us, these consequences are so serious, so far-reaching and pervading, so great a departure from the structure and spirit of our institutions; when the effect is to fetter and degrade the State governments by subjecting them to the control of Congress, in the exercise of powers heretofore universally conceded to them of the most ordinary and fundamental character; when in fact it radically changes the whole theory of the relations of the State and Federal governments to each other and of both these governments to the people; the argument has a force that is irresistible, in the absence of language which expresses such a purpose too clearly to admit of doubt.

We are convinced that no such results were intended by the Congress which proposed these amendments, nor by the legislatures of the States which ratified them.

Having shown that the privileges and immunities relied on in the argument are those which belong to citizens of the States as such, and that they are left to the State governments for security and protection, and not by this article placed under the special care of the Federal government, we may hold ourselves excused from defining the privileges and immunities of citizens of the United States which no State can abridge, until some case involving those privileges may make it necessary to do so.

But lest it should be said that no such privileges and immunities are to be found if those we have been considering are excluded, we venture to suggest some which owe their existence to the Federal government, its National character, its Constitution, or its laws.

One of these is well described in the case of *Crandall v. Nevada.* It is said to be the right of the citizen of this great country, protected by implied guarantees of its Constitution, "to come to the seat of government to assert any claim he may have upon that government, to transact any business he may have with it, to seek its protection, to share its offices, to engage in administering its functions. He has the right of free access to its seaports, through which all operations of foreign commerce are conducted, to the sub-treasuries, land offices, and courts of justice in the several States." And quoting from the language of Chief Justice Taney in another case, it is said "that *for all the great purposes for which the Federal government* was established, we are one people, with one common country, *we are all citizens of the United States,*" and it is, as such citizens, that their rights are supported in this court in *Crandall v. Nevada.*

Another privilege of a citizen of the United States is to demand the care and protection of the Federal government over his life, liberty, and property when on the high seas or within the jurisdiction of a foreign government. Of this there can be no doubt, nor that the right depends upon his character as a citizen of the United States. The right to peaceably assemble and petition for redress of grievances, the privileges of the writ of *habeas corpus*, are rights of the citizen guaranteed by the Federal Constitution. The right to use the navigable waters of the United States, however they may penetrate the territory of the several States, all rights secured to our citizens by treaties with foreign nations, are dependent upon citizenship of the United States, and not citizenship of a State. One of these privileges is conferred by the very article under consideration. It is that a citizen of the United States can, of his own volition, become a citizen of any State of the Union by a *bona fide* residence therein, with the same rights as other citizens of that State. To these may be added the rights secured by the thirteenth and fifteenth articles of amendment, and by the other clause of the fourteenth, next to be considered.

But it is useless to pursue this branch of the inquiry, since we are of opinion that the rights claimed by [the Butchers' Benevolent Association], if they have any existence, are not privileges and immunities of citizens of the United States within the meaning of the clause of the fourteenth amendment under consideration.

"All persons born or naturalized in the United States, and subject to the jurisdiction thereof, are citizens of the United States and of the State wherein they reside. No State shall make or enforce any law which shall abridge the privileges

or immunities of citizens of the United States;
nor shall any State deprive any person of life, liberty, or property without due process of law, nor
deny to any person within its jurisdiction the
equal protection of its laws."

The argument has not been much pressed in these cases
that the [Slaughterhouse]'s charter deprives the [Butchers'
Benevolent Association] of their property without due
process of law, or that it denies to them the equal protection of the law. The first of these paragraphs has been in
the Constitution since the adoption of the fifth amendment, as a restraint upon the Federal power. It is also to
be found in some form of expression in the constitutions
of nearly all the States, as a restraint upon the power of
the States. This law, then, has practically been the same as
it now is during the existence of the government, except
so far as the present amendment may place the restraining
power over the States in this matter in the hands of the
Federal government.

We are not without judicial interpretation, therefore, both
State and National, of the meaning of this clause. And it
is sufficient to say that under no construction of that provision that we have ever seen, or any that we deem admis-
sible, can the restraint imposed by the State of Louisiana
upon the exercise of their trade by the butchers of New
Orleans be held to be a deprivation of property within the
meaning of that provision.

"Nor shall any State deny to any person within its
jurisdiction the equal protection of the laws."

In the light of the history of these amendments, and the
pervading purpose of them, which we have already dis-

cussed, it is not difficult to give a meaning to this clause. The existence of laws in the States where the newly emancipated negroes resided, which discriminated with gross injustice and hardship against them as a class, was the evil to be remedied by this clause, and by it such laws are forbidden.

If, however, the States did not conform their laws to its requirements, then by the fifth section of the article of amendment Congress was authorized to enforce it by suitable legislation. We doubt very much whether any action of a State not directed by way of discrimination against the negroes as a class, or on account of their race, will ever be held to come within the purview of this provision. It is so clearly a provision for that race and that emergency, that a strong case would be necessary for its application to any other. But as it is a State that is to be dealt with, and not alone the validity of its laws, we may safely leave that matter until Congress shall have exercised its power, or some case of State oppression, by denial of equal justice in its courts, shall have claimed a decision at our hands. We find no such case in the one before us, and do not deem it necessary to go over the argument again, as it may have relation to this particular clause of the amendment.

In the early history of the organization of the government, its statesmen seem to have divided on the line which should separate the powers of the National government from those of the State governments, and though this line has never been very well defined in public opinion, such a division has continued from that day to this.

The adoption of the first eleven amendments to the Constitution so soon after the original instrument was accepted, shows a prevailing sense of danger at that time from the Federal power. And it cannot be denied that such a jealousy continued to exist with many patriotic men until the breaking out of the late civil war. It was then discovered that the true danger to the perpetuity of the Union was in the capacity of the State organizations to combine and concentrate all the powers of the State, and of contiguous States, for a determined resistance to the General Government.

Unquestionably this has given great force to the argument, and added largely to the number of those who believe in the necessity of a strong National government.

But, however pervading this sentiment, and however it may have contributed to the adoption of the amendments we have been considering, we do not see in those amendments any purpose to destroy the main features of the general system. Under the pressure of all the excited feeling growing out of the war, our statesmen have still believed that the existence of the States with powers for domestic and local government, including the regulation of civil rights - the rights of person and of property - was essential to the perfect working of our complex form of government, though they have thought proper to impose additional limitations on the States, and to confer additional power on that of the Nation.

But whatever fluctuations may be seen in the history of public opinion on this subject during the period of our national existence, we think it will be found that this court, so far as its functions required, has always held with a steady and an even hand the balance between State and Federal power, and we trust that such may continue to be the history of its relation to that subject so long as it shall have duties to perform which demand of it a construction of the Constitution, or of any of its parts.

The judgments of the Supreme Court of Louisiana in these cases are affirmed [upheld].

The Slaughterhouse Cases *effectively emasculated the Fourteenth Amendment's Privileges or Immunities Clause. The Privileges or Immunities Clause was never again used to protect civil rights.*

Ten years later the Louisiana Legislature repealed the monopoly they had granted to the Crescent City Slaughter House Company. The United States Supreme Court unanimously upheld that repeal in 1884.

THE SEGREGATION CASES

The Civil Rights Cases

That all persons within the jurisdiction of the United States shall be entitled to the full and equal enjoyment of the accommodations, advantages, facilities, and privileges of inns, public conveyances on land or water, theatres, and other places of public amusement . . . applicable alike to all citizens of every race and color, regardless of any previous condition of servitude.

The Civil Rights Act of 1875

On March 1, 1875 the United States Congress passed an antidiscrimination law entitled "An Act to protect all citizens in their civil and legal rights." The Civil Rights Act of 1875 prohibited acts of racial discrimination in the private sector by the owners of all hotels, restaurants, theatres, railroads, and steamships which served the public. Congress asserted the constitutional authority to enact this equal access law under the provisions of the Thirteenth and Fourteenth Amendments.

Five individual challenges to the constitutionality of the Civil Rights Act of 1875, known collectively as the Civil Rights Cases, reached the Supreme Court in 1882 and were decided together in 1883. Individually the Civil Rights Cases were: *United States v. Stanley,* an appeal from the Federal Circuit Court for the District of Kansas; *United States v. Ryan,* an appeal from the Federal Circuit Court for the District of California; *United States v. Nichols,* an appeal from the Federal Circuit Court for the District of Missouri; *United States v. Singleton,* an appeal from the Federal Circuit Court of New York; and *Robinson v. Memphis Railroad,* an appeal from the Federal Circuit Court of Tennessee.

On October 15, 1883 Justice Joseph Bradley announced the 8-1 decision of the Court. The edited text follows.

THE CIVIL RIGHTS COURT

Chief Justice Morrison Waite
Appointed by President Grant
Served 1874 - 1888

Associate Justice Samuel Miller
Appointed by President Lincoln
Served 1862 - 1890

Associate Justice Stephen Field
Appointed by President Lincoln
Served 1863 - 1897

Associate Justice Joseph Bradley
Appointed by President Grant
Served 1870 - 1892

Associate Justice John Marshall Harlan
Appointed by President Hayes
Served 1877 - 1911

Associate Justice William Woods
Appointed by President Hayes
Served 1880 - 1887

Associate Justice Stanley Matthews
Appointed by President Garfield
Served 1881 - 1889

Associate Justice Horace Gray
Appointed by President Arthur
Served 1881 - 1902

Associate Justice Samuel Blatchford
Appointed by President Arthur
Served 1882 - 1893

The unedited text of *The Civil Rights Cases* can be found
on page 3, volume 109 of *United States Reports.*

THE CIVIL RIGHTS CASES
October 15, 1883

JUSTICE BRADLEY: It is obvious that the primary and important question in all the cases is the constitutionality of the [Civil Rights Act of 1875]: for if the law is unconstitutional none of the prosecutions can stand.

The sections of the law referred to provide as follows:

"Sec. 1. That all persons within the jurisdiction of the United States shall be entitled to the full and equal enjoyment of the accommodations, advantages, facilities, and privileges of inns, public conveyances on land or water, theatres, and other places of public amusement; subject only to the conditions and limitations established by law, and applicable alike to citizens of every race and color, regardless of any previous condition of servitude.

"Sec. 2. That any person who shall violate the foregoing section by denying to any citizen, except for reasons by law applicable to citizens of every race and color, and regardless of any previous condition of servitude, the full enjoyment of any of the accommodations, advantages, facilities, or privileges in said section enumerated, or by aiding or inciting such denial, shall for every such offence forfeit and pay the sum of five hundred dollars to the person aggrieved thereby, to be recovered in an action of debt, with full costs; and shall also, for every such offence, be deemed guilty of a misdemeanor, and, upon conviction thereof, shall be fined not less than five hundred nor more than one thousand dollars, or shall be imprisoned not less than thirty days nor more than one year: *Provided*, That all persons may elect to sue for the penalty aforesaid, or to proceed under their rights at common law and by State statutes; and having so elected to proceed in the one mode or the other, their right to proceed in the other jurisdiction shall be barred. But this provision shall not apply to criminal proceedings, either under this act or the criminal law of any State: *And provided further*, That a judgment for the penalty in favor of the party aggrieved, or a judgment upon an indictment [a charge], shall be a bar to either prosecution respectively."

Are these sections constitutional? The first section, which is the principal one, cannot be fairly understood without attending to the last clause, which qualifies the preceding part.

The essence of the law is, not to declare broadly that all persons shall be entitled to the full and equal enjoyment of the accommodations, advantages, facilities, and privileges of inns, public conveyances, and theatres; but that such enjoyment shall not be subject to any conditions applicable only to citizens of a particular race or color, or who had been in a previous condition of servitude. In other words, it is the purpose of the law to declare that, in the enjoyment of the accommodations and privileges of inns, public conveyances, theatres, and other places of public amusement, no distinction shall be made between citizens of different race or color, or between those who have, and those who have not, been slaves. Its effect is to declare, that in all inns, public conveyances, and places of amusement, colored citizens, whether formerly slaves or not, and citizens of other races, shall have the same accommodations and privileges in all inns, public conveyances, and places of amusement as are enjoyed by white citizens; and *vice versa.* The second section makes it a penal offence in any person to deny to any citizen of any race or color, regardless of previous servitude, any of the accommodations or privileges mentioned in the first section.

Has Congress constitutional power to make such a law? Of course, no one will contend that the power to pass it was contained in the Constitution before the adoption of the last three amendments. The power is sought, first, in the Fourteenth Amendment, and the views and arguments of distinguished Senators, advanced whilst the law was under consideration, claiming authority to pass it by virtue of that amendment, are the principal arguments adduced in favor of the power. We have carefully considered those arguments, as was due to the eminent ability of those who put them forward, and have felt, in all its force, the weight of authority which always invests a law that Congress deems itself competent to pass. But the responsibility of an independent judgment is now thrown upon this court; and we are bound to exercise it according to the best lights we have.

The first section of the Fourteenth Amendment (which is the one relied on), after declaring who shall be citizens of the United States, and of the several States, is prohibitory in its character, and prohibitory upon the States. It declares that:

> "No State shall make or enforce any law which shall abridge the privileges or immunities of citizens of the United States; nor shall any State de-

prive any person of life, liberty, or property
without due process of law; nor deny to any person within its jurisdiction the equal protection of
the laws."

It is State action of a particular character that is prohibited. Individual invasion of individual rights is not the
subject-matter of the amendment. It has a deeper and
broader scope. It nullifies and makes void all State legislation, and State action of every kind, which impairs the
privileges and immunities of citizens of the United States,
or which injures them in life, liberty or property without
due process of law, or which denies to any of them the
equal protection of the laws. It not only does this, but, in
order that the national will, thus declared, may not be a
mere *brutum fulmen* [empty threat], the last section of
the amendment invests Congress with power to enforce it
by appropriate legislation. To enforce what? To enforce
the prohibition. To adopt appropriate legislation for cor-
recting the effects of such prohibited States laws and
State acts, and thus to render them effectually null, void,
and innocuous. This is the legislative power conferred
upon Congress, and this is the whole of it. It does not invest Congress with power to legislate upon subjects which
are within the domain of State legislation; but to provide
modes of relief against State legislation, or State action, of
the kind referred to. It does not authorize Congress to
create a code of municipal law for the regulation of private rights; but to provide modes of redress against the
operation of State laws, and the action of State officers
executive or judicial, when these are subversive of the
fundamental rights specified in the amendment. Positive
rights and privileges are undoubtedly secured by the
Fourteenth Amendment; but they are secured by way of
prohibition against State laws and State proceedings af-

fecting those rights and privileges, and by power given to Congress to legislate for the purpose of carrying such prohibition into effect: and such legislation must necessarily be predicated upon such supposed State laws or State proceedings, and be directed to the correction of their operation and effect. . . .

An apt illustration of this distinction may be found in some of the provisions of the original Constitution. Take the subject of contracts, for example. The Constitution prohibited the States from passing any law impairing the obligation of contracts. This did not give to Congress power to provide laws for the general enforcement of contracts; nor power to invest the courts of the United States with jurisdiction over contracts, so as to enable parties to sue upon them in those courts. It did, however, give the power to provide remedies by which the impairment of contracts by State legislation might be counteracted and corrected: and this power was exercised. The remedy which Congress actually provided was that contained in the 25th section of the Judiciary Act of 1789, giving to the Supreme Court of the United States jurisdiction . . . to review the final decisions of State courts whenever they should sustain [maintain] the validity of a State statute or authority alleged to be repugnant to the Constitution or laws of the United States. By this means, if a State law was passed impairing the obligation of a contract, and the State tribunals sustained the validity of the law, the mischief could be corrected in this court. The legislation of Congress, and the proceedings provided for under it, were corrective in their character. No attempt was made to draw into the United States courts the litigation of contracts generally; and no such attempt would have been sustained. We do not say that the remedy provided was the only one that might have been provided in that case. Probably Congress had power to pass a law giving to the courts of the United States direct jurisdiction over contracts alleged to be impaired by a State law; and under the broad provisions of the [Civil Rights Act] of March 3d, 1875, giving to the circuit courts jurisdiction of all cases arising under the Constitution and laws of the United States, it is possible that such jurisdiction now exists. But under that, or any other law, it must appear as well by allegation, as proof at the trial, that the Constitution had been violated by the action of the State legislature. Some obnoxious State law passed, or that might be passed, is necessary to be assumed in order to lay the foundation of any federal remedy in the case; and for the very sufficient reason, that the constitutional prohibition is against *State laws* impairing the obligation of contracts.

And so in the present case, until some State law has been passed, or some State action through its officers or agents has been taken, adverse to the rights of citizens sought to be protected by the Fourteenth Amendment, no legislation of the United States under said amendment, nor any proceeding under such legislation, can be called into activity: for the prohibitions of the amendment are against State laws and acts done under State authority. Of course, legislation may, and should be, provided in advance to meet the exigency when it arises; but it should be adapted to the mischief and wrong which the amendment was intended to provide against; and that is, State laws, or State action of some kind, adverse to the rights of the citizen secured by the amendment. Such legislation cannot properly cover the whole domain of rights appertaining to life, liberty and property, defining them and providing for their vindication. That would be to establish a code of municipal law regulative of all private rights between man and man in society. It would be to make Congress take the place of the State legislatures and to supersede them. It is absurd to affirm [uphold] that, because the rights of life, liberty and property (which include all civil rights that men have), are by the amendment sought to be protected against invasion on the part of the State without due process of law, Congress may therefore provide due process of law for their vindication in every case; and that, because the denial by a State to any persons, of the equal protection of the laws, is prohibited by the amendment, therefore Congress may establish laws for their equal protection. In fine, the legislation which Congress is authorized to adopt in this behalf is not general legislation upon the rights of the citizen, but corrective legislation, that is, such as may be necessary and proper for counteracting such laws as the States may adopt or enforce, and which, by the amendment, they are prohibited from making or enforcing, or such acts and proceedings as the States may commit or take, and which, by the amendment, they are prohibited from committing or taking. It is not necessary for us to state, if we could, what legislation would be proper for Congress to adopt. It is sufficient for us to examine whether the law in question is of that character.

An inspection of the law shows that it makes no reference whatever to any supposed or apprehended violation of the Fourteenth Amendment on the part of the States. It is not predicated on any such view. It proceeds . . . to declare that certain acts committed by individuals shall be deemed offences, and shall be prosecuted and punished by proceedings in the courts of the United States. It does not profess to be corrective of any constitutional wrong committed by the States; it does not make its operation to depend upon any such wrong committed. It applies equally to cases arising in States which have the justest laws respecting the personal rights of citizens, and whose authorities are ever ready to enforce such laws, as to those which arise in States that may have violated the prohibition of the amendment. In other words, it steps into the domain of local jurisprudence [the science of law], and lays down rules for the conduct of individuals in society towards each other, and imposes sanctions for the enforcement of those rules, without referring in any manner to any supposed action of the State or its authorities.

If this legislation is appropriate for enforcing the prohibitions of the amendment, it is difficult to see where it is to stop. Why may not Congress with equal show of authority enact a code of laws for the enforcement and vindication of all rights of life, liberty, and property? If it is supposable that the States may deprive persons of life, liberty, and property without due process of law (and the amendment itself does suppose this), why should not Congress proceed at once to prescribe due process of law for the protection of every one of these fundamental rights, in every possible case, as well as to prescribe equal privileges in inns, public conveyances, and theatres? The truth is, that the implication of a power to legislate in this manner is based upon the assumption that if the States are forbidden to legislate or act in a particular way on a particular subject, and power is conferred upon Congress to enforce the prohibition, this gives Congress power to legislate generally upon that subject, and not merely power to provide modes of redress against such State legislation or action. The assumption is certainly unsound. It is repugnant to the Tenth Amendment of the Constitution, which declares that powers not delegated to the United States by the Constitution, nor prohibited by it to the States, are reserved to the States respectively or to the people.

We have not overlooked the fact that the fourth section of the act now under consideration has been held by this court to be constitutional. That section declares "that no citizen, possessing all other qualifications which are or may be prescribed by law, shall be disqualified for service as grand or petit juror in any court of the United States, or of any State, on account of race, color, or previous condition of servitude; and any officer or other person charged with any duty in the selection or summoning of jurors who shall exclude or fail to summon any citizen for the cause aforesaid, shall, on conviction thereof, be deemed guilty of a misdemeanor, and be fined not more than five thousand dollars." In *Ex parte Virginia*, it was held that an indictment [a charge] against a State officer under this section for excluding persons of color from the jury list is sustainable. But a moment's attention to its terms will show that the section is entirely corrective in its character. Disqualifications for service on juries are only created by the law, and the first part of the section is aimed at certain disqualifying laws, namely, those which make mere race or color a disqualification; and the second clause is directed against those who, assuming to use the authority of the State government, carry into effect such a rule of disqualification. In the Virginia case, the State, through its officer, enforced a rule of disqualification which the law was intended to abrogate and counteract. Whether the statute book of the State actually laid down any such rule of disqualification, or not, the State, through its officer, enforced such a rule: and it is against such State action, through its officers and agents, that the last clause of the section is directed. This aspect of the law was deemed sufficient to divest it of any unconstitutional character, and makes it differ widely from the first and second sections of the same act which we are now considering.

These sections, in the objectionable features before referred to, are different also from the law ordinarily called the "Civil Rights Bill," originally passed April 9th, 1866, and re-enacted with some modifications in sections 16, 17, 18, of the Enforcement Act, passed May 31st, 1870. That law, as re-enacted, after declaring that all persons within the jurisdiction of the United States shall have the same right in every State and Territory to make and enforce contracts, to sue, be parties, give evidence, and to the full and equal benefit of all laws and proceedings for the security of persons and property as is enjoyed by white citizens, and shall be subject to like punishment, pains, penalties, taxes, licenses and exactions of every kind, and none other, any law, statute, ordinance, regulation or custom to the contrary notwithstanding, proceeds to enact, that any person who, under color of any law, statute, ordinance, regulation or custom, shall subject, or cause to be subjected, any inhabitant of any State or Territory to the deprivation of any rights secured or protected by the preceding section . . . , or to different punishment, pains, or penalties, on account of such person being an alien, or by reason of his color or race, than is prescribed for the punishment of citizens, shall be deemed guilty of a misdemeanor [a crime less than a felony], and subject to fine and imprisonment as specified in the act. This law is clearly corrective in its character, intended to counteract and furnish redress against State laws and proceedings, and customs having the force of law, which sanction the wrongful acts specified. In the Revised Statutes, it is true, a very important clause, to wit, the words "any law, statute, ordinance, regulation or custom to the contrary notwithstanding," which gave the declaratory section its point and effect, are omitted; but the penal part, by which the declaration is enforced, and which is really the effective part of the law, retains the reference to State laws, by making the penalty apply only to those who should subject parties to a deprivation of their rights under color of any statute, ordinance, custom, etc., of any State or Territory: thus preserving the corrective character of the legislation. The Civil Rights Bill here referred to is analogous in its character to what a law would have been under the original Constitution, declaring that the validity of contracts should not be impaired, and that if any person bound by a contract should refuse to comply with it, under color or pretence that it had been rendered void or invalid by a State law, he should be liable to an action upon it in the courts of the United States, with the addition of a penalty for setting up such an unjust and unconstitutional defence.

In this connection it is proper to state that civil rights, such as are guaranteed by the Constitution against State aggression, cannot be impaired by the wrongful acts of individuals, unsupported by State authority in the shape of laws, customs, or judicial or executive proceedings. The wrongful act of an individual, unsupported by any such authority, is simply a private wrong, or a crime of that individual; an invasion of the rights of the injured party, it is true, whether they affect his person, his property, or his reputation; but if not sanctioned in some way by the State, or not done under State authority, his rights remain in full force, and may presumably be vindicated by resort to the laws of the State for redress. An individual cannot deprive a man of his right to vote, to hold property, to buy and sell, to sue in the courts, or to to be a witness or a juror; he may, by force or fraud, interfere with the enjoyment of the right in a particular case; he may commit an assault against the person, or commit murder, or use ruffian violence at the polls, or slander the good name of a fellow citizen; but, unless protected in these wrongful acts by some shield of State law or State authority, he cannot destroy or injure the right; he will only render himself amenable to satisfaction or punishment; and amenable therefor to the laws of the State where the wrongful acts are committed. Hence, in all those cases where the Constitution seeks to protect the rights of the citizen against discriminative and unjust laws of the State by prohibiting such laws, it is not individual offences, but abrogation [cancellation] and denial of rights, which it denounces, and for which it clothes the Congress with power to provide a remedy. This abrogation and denial of rights, for which the States alone were or could be responsible, was the great seminal and fundamental wrong which was intended to be remedied. And the remedy to be provided must necessarily be predicated upon that wrong. It must assume that in the cases provided for, the evil or wrong actually committed rests upon some State law or State authority for its excuse and perpetration.

Of course, these remarks do not apply to those cases in which Congress is clothed with direct and plenary [broad] powers of legislation over the whole subject, accompanied with an express or implied denial of such power to the States, as in the regulation of commerce with foreign nations, among the several States, and with the Indian tribes, the coining of money, the establishment of post offices and post roads, the declaring of war, etc. In these cases Congress has power to pass laws for regulating the subjects specified in every detail, and the conduct and transactions of individuals in respect thereof. But where a subject is not submitted to the general legislative power of Congress, but is only submitted thereto for the purpose of rendering effective some prohibition against particular State legislation or State action in reference to that subject, the power given is limited by its object, and any legislation by Congress in the matter must necessarily be corrective in its character, adapted to counteract and redress the operation of such prohibited State laws or proceedings of State officers.'

If the principles of interpretation which we have laid down are correct, as we deem them to be . . . , it is clear that the law in question cannot be sustained by any grant of legislative power made to Congress by the Fourteenth Amendment. That amendment prohibits the States from denying to any person the equal protection of the laws, and declares that Congress shall have power to enforce, by appropriate legislation, the provisions of the amendment. The law in question, without any reference to adverse State legislation on the subject, declares that all persons shall be entitled to equal accommodations and privileges of inns, public conveyances, and places of public amusement, and imposes a penalty upon any individual who shall deny to any citizen such equal accommodations and privileges. This is not corrective legislation; it is primary and direct; it takes immediate and absolute possession of the subject of the right of admission to inns, public conveyances, and places of amusement. It supersedes and displaces State legislation on the same subject, or only allows it permissive force. It ignores such legislation, and assumes that the matter is one that belongs to the domain of national regulation. Whether it would not have been a more effective protection of the rights of citizens to have clothed Congress with plenary [broad] power over the whole subject, is not now the question. What we have to decide is, whether such plenary power has been conferred upon Congress by the Fourteenth Amendment; and, in our judgment, it has not.

We have discussed the question presented by the law on the assumption that a right to enjoy equal accommodation and privileges in all inns, public conveyances, and places of public amusement, is one of the essential rights of the citizen which no State can abridge or interfere with. Whether it is such a right, or not, is a different question which, in the view we have taken of the validity of the law on the ground already stated, it is not necessary to examine.

We have also discussed the validity of the law in reference to cases arising in the States only; and not in reference to cases arising in the Territories or the District of Columbia, which are subject to the plenary legislation of Congress in every branch of municipal regulation. Whether the law would be a valid one as applied to the Territories and the District is not a question for consideration in the cases before us; they all being cases arising within the limits of States. And whether Congress, in the exercise of its power to regulate commerce amongst the several States, might or might not pass a law regulating rights in public conveyances passing from one State to another, is also a question which is not now before us, as the sections in question are not conceived in any such view.

But the power of Congress to adopt direct and primary, as distinguished from corrective legislation, on the subject in hand, is sought, in the second place, from the Thirteenth Amendment, which abolishes slavery. This amendment declares "that neither slavery, nor involuntary servitude, except as punishment for crime, whereof the party shall have been duly convicted, shall exist within the United States, or any place subject to their jurisdiction;" and it gives Congress power to enforce the amendment by appropriate legislation.

This amendment, as well as the Fourteenth, is undoubtedly self-executing without any ancillary legislation, so far as its terms are applicable to any existing state of circumstances. By its own unaided force and effect it abolished slavery, and established universal freedom. Still, legislation may be necessary and proper to meet all the various cases and circumstances to be affected by it, and to prescribe proper modes of redress for its violation in letter or spirit. And such legislation may be primary and direct in its character; for the amendment is not a mere prohibition of State laws establishing or upholding slavery, but an absolute declaration that slavery or involuntary servitude shall not exist in any part of the United States.

It is true, that slavery cannot exist without law, any more than property in lands and goods can exist without law: and, therefore, the Thirteenth Amendment may be regarded as nullifying all State laws which establish or uphold slavery. But it has a reflex character also, establishing and decreeing universal civil and political freedom throughout the United States; and it is assumed, that the power vested in Congress to enforce the article by appropriate legislation, clothes Congress with power to pass all laws necessary and proper for abolishing all badges and incidents of slavery in the United States: and upon this assumption it is claimed, that this is sufficient authority for declaring by law that all persons shall have equal accommodations and privileges in all inns, public conveyances, and places of amusement; the argument being, that the denial of such equal accommodations and privileges is, in itself, a subjection to a species of servitude within the meaning of the amendment. Conceding the major proposition to be true, that Congress has a right to enact all necessary and proper laws for the obliteration and prevention of slavery with all its badges and incidents, is the minor proposition also true, that the denial to any person of admission to the accommodations and privileges of an inn, a public conveyance, or a theatre, does subject that person to any form of servitude, or tend to fasten upon him any badge of slavery? If it does not, then power to pass the law is not found in the Thirteenth Amendment.

In a very able and learned presentation of the cognate question as to the extent of the rights, privileges and immunities of citizens which cannot rightfully be abridged by state laws under the Fourteenth Amendment, made in a former case, a long list of burdens and disabilities of a servile character, incident to feudal vassalage in France, and which were abolished by the decrees of the National Assembly, was presented for the purpose of showing that all inequalities and observances exacted by one man from another were servitudes, or badges of slavery, which a great nation, in its effort to establish universal liberty, made haste to wipe out and destroy. But these were servitudes imposed by the old law, or by long custom, which had the force of law, and exacted by one man from another without the latter's consent. Should any such servitudes be imposed by a state law, there can be no doubt that the law would be repugnant to the Fourteenth, no less than to the Thirteenth Amendment; nor any greater doubt that Congress has adequate power to forbid any such servitude from being exacted.

But is there any similarity between such servitudes and a denial by the owner of an inn, a public conveyance, or a theatre, of its accommodations and privileges to an individual, even though the denial be founded on the race or color of that individual? Where does any slavery or servitude, or badge of either, arise from such an act of denial? Whether it might not be a denial of a right which, if sanctioned by the state law, would be obnoxious to the prohibitions of the Fourteenth Amendment, is another question. But what has it to do with the question of slavery?

It may be that by the Black Code (as it was called), in the times when slavery prevailed, the proprietors of inns and public conveyances were forbidden to receive persons of the African race, because it might assist slaves to escape from the control of their masters. This was merely a means of preventing such escapes, and was no part of the servitude itself. A law of that kind could not have any such object now, however justly it might be deemed an invasion of the party's legal right as a citizen, and amenable to the prohibitions of the Fourteenth Amendment.

The long existence of African slavery in this country gave us very distinct notions of what it was, and what were its necessary incidents. Compulsory service of the slave for the benefit of the master, restraint of his movements except by the master's will, disability to hold property, to make contracts, to have a standing in court, to be a witness against a white person, and such like burdens and incapacities, were the inseparable incidents of the institution. Severer punishments for crimes were imposed on the slave than on free persons guilty of the same offences. Congress, as we have seen, by the Civil Rights Bill of 1866, passed in view of the Thirteenth Amendment, before the Fourteenth was adopted, undertook to wipe out these burdens and disabilities, the necessary incidents of slavery, constituting its substance and visible form; and to secure to all citizens of every race and color, and without regard to previous servitude, those fundamental rights which are the essence of civil freedom, namely, the same right to make and enforce contracts, to sue, be parties, give evidence, and to inherit, purchase, lease, sell and convey property, as is enjoyed by white citizens. Whether this legislation was fully authorized by the Thirteenth Amendment alone, without the support which it afterward received from the Fourteenth Amendment, after the adoption of which it was re-enacted with some additions, it is not necessary to inquire. It is referred to for the purpose of showing that at that time (in 1866) Congress did not assume, under the authority given by the Thirteenth Amendment, to adjust what may be called the social rights of men and races in the community; but only to declare and vindicate those fundamental rights which appertain to the essence of citizenship, and the enjoyment or deprivation of which constitutes the essential distinction between freedom and slavery.

We must not forget that the province and scope of the Thirteenth and Fourteenth amendments are different; the former simply abolished slavery: the latter prohibited the States from abridging the privileges or immunities of citizens of the United States; from depriving them of life, liberty, or property without due process of law, and from denying to any the equal protection of the laws. The amendments are different, and the powers of Congress under them are different. What Congress has power to do under one, it may not have power to do under the other. Under the Thirteenth Amendment, it has only to do with slavery and its incidents. Under the Fourteenth Amendment, it has power to counteract and render nugatory [invalid] all State laws and proceedings which have the effect to abridge any of the privileges or immunities of citizens of the United States, or to deprive them of life, liberty or property without due process of law, or to deny to any of them the equal protection of the laws. Under the Thirteenth Amendment, the legislation, so far as necessary or proper to eradicate all forms and incidents of slavery and involuntary servitude, may be direct and primary, operating upon the acts of individuals, whether sanctioned by State legislation or not; under the Fourteenth, as we have already shown, it must necessarily be, and can only be, corrective in its character, addressed to counteract and afford relief against State regulations or proceedings.

The only question under the present head, therefore, is, whether the refusal to any persons of the accommodations of an inn, or a public conveyance, or a place of public amusement, by an individual, and without any sanction or support from any State law or regulation, does inflict upon such persons any manner of servitude, or form of slavery, as those terms are understood in this country? Many wrongs may be obnoxious to the prohibitions of the Fourteenth Amendment which are not, in any just sense, incidents or elements of slavery. Such, for example, would be the taking of private property without due process of law; or allowing persons who have committed certain crimes (horse stealing, for example) to be seized and hung by the *posse comitatus* [group of people acting for the sheriff] without regular trial; or denying to any person, or class of persons, the right to pursue any peaceful avocations allowed to others. What is called class legislation would belong to this category, and would be obnoxious to the prohibitions of the Fourteenth Amendment, but would not necessarily be so to the Thirteenth, when not involving the idea of any subjection of one man to another. The Thirteenth Amendment has respect, not to distinctions of race, or class, or color, but to slavery. The Fourteenth Amendment extends its protection to races and classes, and prohibits any State legislation which has the effect of denying to any race or class, or to any individual, the equal protection of the laws.

Now, conceding, for the sake of the argument, that the admission to an inn, a public conveyance, or a place of public amusement, on equal terms with all other citizens, is the right of every man and all classes of men, is it any more than one of those rights which the states by the Fourteenth Amendment are forbidden to deny to any person? And is the Constitution violated until the denial of the right has some State sanction or authority? Can the act of a mere individual, the owner of the inn, the public conveyance or place of amusement, refusing the accommodation, be justly regarded as imposing any badge of slavery or servitude upon the applicant, or only as inflicting an ordinary civil injury, properly cognizable by the laws of the State, and presumably subject to redress by those laws until the contrary appears?

After giving to these questions all the consideration which their importance demands, we are forced to the conclusion that such an act of refusal has nothing to do with slavery or involuntary servitude, and that if it is violative of any right of the party, his redress is to be sought under the laws of the State; or if those laws are adverse to his rights and do not protect him, his remedy will be found in the corrective legislation which Congress has adopted, or may adopt, for counteracting the effect of State laws, or State action, prohibited by the Fourteenth Amendment. It would be running the slavery argument into the ground to make it apply to every act of discrimination which a person may see fit to make as to the guests he will entertain, or as to the people he will take into his coach or cab or car, or admit to his concert or theatre, or deal with in other matters of intercourse or business. Innkeepers and public carriers, by the laws of all the States, so far as we are aware, are bound, to the extent of their facilities, to furnish proper accommodation to all unobjectionable persons who in good faith apply for them. If the laws themselves make any unjust discrimination, amenable to the prohibitions of the Fourteenth Amendment, Congress has full power to afford a remedy under that amendment and in accordance with it.

When a man has emerged from slavery, and by the aid of beneficent legislation has shaken off the inseparable concomitants of that state, there must be some stage in the progress of his elevation when he takes the rank of a mere citizen, and ceases to be the special favorite of the laws, and when his rights as a citizen, or a man, are to be protected in the ordinary modes by which other men's rights are protected. There were thousands of free colored people in this country before the abolition of slavery, enjoying all the essential rights of life, liberty and property the same as white citizens; yet no one, at that time, thought that it was any invasion of his personal status as a freeman because he was not admitted to all the privileges enjoyed by white citizens, or because he was subjected to discriminations in the enjoyment of accommodations in inns, public conveyances and places of amusement. Mere discriminations on account of race or color were not regarded as badges of slavery. If, since that time, the enjoyment of equal rights in all these respects has become established by constitutional enactment, it is not by force of the Thirteenth Amendment (which merely abolishes slavery), but by force of the Thirteenth and Fifteenth Amendments.

On the whole we are of opinion, that no countenance of authority for the passage of the law in question can be found in either the Thirteenth or Fourteenth Amendment of the Constitution; and no other ground of authority for its passage being suggested, it must necessarily be declared void, at least so far as its operation in the several States is concerned.

This conclusion disposes of the cases now under consideration. In the cases of the *United States v. Michael Ryan,* and of *Richard A. Robinson and Wife v. The Memphis & Charleston Railroad Company,* the judgments must be affirmed. In the other cases, the answer to be given will be that the first and second sections of the [Civil Rights Act] of March 1st, 1875, entitled "An Act to protect all citizens in their civil and legal rights," are unconstitutional and void, and that judgment should be rendered upon the several indictments in those cases accordingly.

And it is so ordered.

The Civil Rights Cases, *which severely limited Congress' powers over private discrimination under the Thirteenth and Fourteenth Amendments, were decided by an 8-1 majority. The minority of one was Justice John Marshall Harlan, who wrote in angry dissent: "I insist that the National Legislature may . . . do for human liberty . . . what it did . . . for the protection of slavery and the rights of the masters of fugitive slaves." The legality of private racial discrimination established in the* Civil Rights Cases *was not overruled by the U.S. Supreme Court until 1968.*

THE SEPARATE BUT EQUAL CASE

Plessy v. Ferguson

All railway companies carrying passengers in their coaches in this state shall provide equal but separate accommodations for the white and colored races.

An Act of Louisiana, July 10, 1890

In the post-Civil War South "Jim Crow" segregation laws were enacted by several southern states to counter the integration effects of the Thirteenth and Fourteenth Amendments to the United States Constitution.

In 1890 Louisiana enacted a "Jim Crow" law providing separate railway carriages for white and colored races. On June 7, 1892 Homer Adolph Plessy, a Louisianian of mixed descent, seven-eighths Caucasian and one-eighth African, purchased a first class ticket in New Orleans on the East Louisiana Railway. Plessy, whose African descent was said not to be discernable in him, took a seat in a Whites-Only passenger coach. The conductor, told of Plessy's African descent, ordered Plessy to a Colored-Only coach. Plessy refused. The police were called. Plessy was ejected from the train and imprisoned for violation of Louisiana's "Jim Crow" law of July 10, 1890. Plessy, brought before John H. Ferguson, Judge of the Criminal Court for the Parish of Orleans, refused either to plead or to identify his race, asserting the July 10th law was an unconstitutional act. Plessy filed a petition to prohibit further proceedings by Judge Ferguson. The Louisiana Supreme Court held for the Judge. Homer Plessy appealed to the United States Supreme Court.

On May 18, 1896 Justice Henry Brown announced the 8-1 decision of the Court. The edited text follows.

THE PLESSY COURT

Chief Justice Melville W. Fuller
Appointed by President Cleveland
Served 1888 - 1901

Associate Justice Stephen J. Field
Appointed by President Lincoln
Served 1863 - 1897

Associate Justice John Marshall Harlan
Appointed by President Hayes
Served 1877 - 1911

Associate Justice Horace Grey
Appointed by President Arthur
Served 1881- 1902

Associate Justice Henry B. Brown
Appointed by President Harrison
Served 1890 - 1906

Associate Justice George Shiras, Jr.
Appointed by President Harrison
Served 1892 - 1903

Associate Justice Edward D. White
Appointed Associate Justice by President Cleveland
Appointed Chief Justice by President Taft
Served 1894 - 1921

Associate Justice Rufus W. Peckham
Appointed by President Cleveland
Served 1895 - 1909

The unedited text of *Plessy v. Ferguson* can be found
on page 537, volume 163 of *United States Reports.*

PLESSY v. FERGUSON
May 18, 1896

JUSTICE BROWN: This case turns upon the constitutionality of an act of the general assembly of the state of Louisiana, passed in 1890, providing for separate railway carriages for the white and colored races.

The 1st section of the statute enacts "that all railway companies carrying passengers in their coaches in this state shall provide equal but separate accommodations for the white and colored races, by providing two or more passenger coaches for each passenger train, or by dividing the passenger coaches by a partition so as to secure separate accommodations: *Provided*, That this section shall not be construed [interpreted] to apply to street railroads. No person or persons shall be permitted to occupy seats in coaches other than the ones assigned to them, on account of the race they belong to."

By the 2d section it was enacted "that the officers of such passenger trains shall have power and are hereby required to assign each passenger to the coach or compartment used for the race to which such passenger belongs; any passenger insisting on going into a coach or compartment to which by race he does not belong, shall be liable to a fine of $25 or in lieu thereof to imprisonment for a period of not more than twenty days in the parish prison, and any officer of any railroad insisting on assigning a passenger to a coach or compartment other than the one set aside for the race to which said passenger belongs, shall be liable to a fine of $25, or in lieu thereof to imprisonment for a period of not more than twenty days in the parish prison; and should any passenger refuse to occupy the coach or compartment to which he or she is assigned by

the officer of such railway, said officer shall have power
to refuse to carry such passenger on his train, and for
such refusal neither he nor the railway company which he
represents shall be liable for damages in any of the courts
of this state."

The 3d section provides penalties for the refusal or ne-
glect of the officers, directors, conductors, and employees
of railway companies to comply with the act, with a
proviso that "nothing in this act shall be construed as applying to nurses attending children of the other race." . . .

The information filed in the criminal district court
charged in substance that Plessy, being a passenger between two stations within the state of Louisiana, was assigned by officers of the company to the coach used for
the race to which he belonged, but he insisted upon going
into a coach used by the race to which he did not belong.
[Nowhere] was his particular race or color [indicated].

The petition [request to the court] . . . averred [declared]
that petitioner [Plessy] was seven eighths Caucasian and
one eighth African blood; that the mixture of colored
blood was not discernible in him, and that he was entitled
to every right, privilege, and immunity secured to citizens
of the United States of the white race; and that, upon such
theory, he took a possession of a vacant seat in a coach
where passengers of the white race were accommodated,
and was ordered by the conductor to vacate said coach and
take a seat in another assigned to persons of the colored
race, and having refused to comply with such demand he
was forcibly ejected with the aid of a police officer, and
imprisoned in the parish jail to answer a charge of having
violated the above act.

The constitutionality of this act is attacked upon the ground that it conflicts both with the 13th Amendment of the Constitution, abolishing slavery, and the 14th Amendment, which prohibits certain restrictive legislation on the part of the states.

That it does not conflict with the 13th Amendment,which abolished slavery and involuntary servitude, except as a punishment for crime, is too clear for argument. Slavery implies involuntary servitude - a state of bondage; the ownership of mankind as a chattel, or at least the control of the labor and services of one man for the benefit of another, and the absence of a legal right to the disposal of his own person, property, and services. This amendment was said in *Butcher's Benevolent Association v. Crescent City Slaughter House ("Slaughterhouse Cases")*, to have been intended primarily to abolish slavery, as it had been previously known in this country, and that it equally forbade Mexican peonage or the Chinese coolie trade when they amounted to slavery or involuntary servitude, and that the use of the word "servitude" was intended to prohibit the use of all forms of involuntary slavery, of whatever class or name. It was intimated, however, in that case, that this amendment was regarded by the statesmen of that day as insufficient to protect the colored race from certain laws which had been enacted in the southern states, imposing upon the colored race onerous disabilities and burdens, and curtailing their rights in the pursuit of life, liberty, and property to such an extent that their freedom was of little value; and that the 14th Amendment was devised to meet this exigency.

So, too, in *United States v. Stanley ("Civil Rights Cases")*, it was said that the act of a mere individual, the owner of an inn, a public conveyance, or place of amusement, refusing accommodations to colored people, cannot be justly regarded as imposing any badge of slavery or servitude upon the applicant, but only as involving an ordinary civil injury, properly cognizable by the laws of the state, and presumably subject to redress by those laws until the contrary appears. "It would be running the slavery argument into the ground," said Justice Bradley, "to make it apply to every act of discrimination which a person may see fit to make as to the guests he will entertain, or as to the people he will take into his coach or cab or car, or admit to his concert or theater, or deal with in other matters of intercourse or business."

A statute which implies merely a legal distinction between the white and colored races - a distinction which is founded in the color of the two races, and which must always exist so long as white men are distinguished from the other race by color - has no tendency to destroy the legal equality of the two races, or reestablish a state of involuntary servitude. Indeed, we do not understand that the 13th Amendment is strenuously relied upon by [Plessy] in this connection.

By the 14th Amendment, all persons born or naturalized in the United States, and subject to the jurisdiction thereof, are made citizens of the United States, and of the state wherein they reside; and the states are forbidden from making or enforcing any law which shall abridge the privileges or immunities of citizens of the United States, or shall deprive any person of life, liberty, or property without due process of law, or deny to any person within their jurisdiction the equal protection of the laws.

The proper construction of this amendment was first called to the attention of this court in the *Slaughterhouse*

Cases, which involved, however, not a question of race, but one of exclusive privileges. The case did not call for any expression of opinion as to the exact rights it was intended to secure to the colored race, but it was said generally that its main purpose was to establish the citizenship of the negro; to give definitions of citizenship of the United States and of the states, and to protect from the hostile legislation of the states the privileges and immunities of citizens of the United States, as distinguished from those of citizens of the states.

The object of the amendment was undoubtedly to enforce the absolute equality of the two races before the law, but in the nature of things it could not have been intended to abolish distinctions based upon color, or to enforce social, as distinguished from political, equality, or a commingling of the two races upon terms unsatisfactory to either. Laws permitting, and even requiring their separation in places where they are liable to be brought into contact do not necessarily imply the inferiority of either race to the other, and have been generally, if not universally, recognized as within the competency of the state legislatures in the exercise of their police power. The most common instance of this is connected with the establishment of separate schools for white and colored children, which have been held to be a valid exercise of the legislative power even by courts of states where the political rights of the colored race have been longest and most earnestly enforced.

One of the earliest of these cases is that of *Roberts v. Boston,* in which the supreme judicial court of Massachusetts held that the general school committee of Boston had power to make provision for the instruction of colored children in separate schools established exclusively for them, and to prohibit their attendance upon the other schools. "The great principle," said Chief Justice Shaw, "advanced by the learned and eloquent advocate of the plaintiff [Mr. Charles Sumner] is, that by the Constitution and laws of Massachusetts, all persons without distinction of age or sex, birth or color, origin or condition, are equal before the law. . . . But, when this great principle comes to be applied to the actual and various conditions of persons in society, it will not warrant the assertion that men and women are legally clothed with the same civil and political powers, and that children and adults are legally to have the same functions and be subject to the same treatment; but only that the rights of all, as they are settled and regulated by law, are equally entitled to the paternal consideration and protection of the law for their maintenance and security." It was held that the powers of the committee extended to the "establishment of separate schools for children of different ages, sexes, and colors, and that they might also establish special schools for poor and neglected children, who have become too old to attend the primary school, and yet have not acquired the rudiments of learning, to enable them to enter the ordinary schools. Similar laws have been enacted by Congress under its general power of legislation over the District of Columbia, as well as by the legislatures of many of the states, and have been generally, if not uniformly, sustained [maintained] by the courts.

Laws forbidding the intermarriage of the two races may be said in a technical sense to interfere with the freedom of contract, and yet have been universally recognized as within the police power of the state.

The distinction between laws interfering with the political equality of the negro and those requiring the separation of the two races in schools, theaters, and railway carriages, has been frequently drawn by this court. Thus, in *Strauder v. West Virginia*, it was held that a law of West Virginia limiting to white male persons, twenty-one years of age and citizens of the state, the right to sit upon juries, was a discrimination which implied a legal inferiority in civil society, which lessened the security of the right of the colored race, and was a step towards reducing them to a condition of servility. Indeed, the right of a colored man that, in the selection of jurors to pass upon his life, liberty, and property, there shall be no exclusion of his race and no discrimination against them because of color, has been asserted in a number of cases. So, where the laws of a particular locality or the charter of a particular railway corporation has provided that no person shall be excluded from the cars on account of color, we have held that this meant that persons of color should travel in the same car as white ones, and that the enactment was not satisfied by the company providing cars assigned exclusively to people of color, though they were as good as those which they assigned exclusively to white persons.

Upon the other hand, where a statute of Louisiana required those engaged in the transportation of passengers among the states to give to all persons traveling within that state, upon vessels employed in that business, equal rights and privileges in all parts of the vessel, without distinction on account of race or color, and subjected to an action for damages, the owner of such a vessel, who excluded colored passengers on account of their color from the cabin set aside by him for the use of whites, it was held to be, so far as it applied to interstate commerce, unconstitutional and void. The court in this case, however, expressly disclaimed that it had anything whatever to do with the statute as a regulation of internal commerce, or affecting anything else than commerce among the states.

In *United States v. Stanley*, it was held that an act of Congress, entitling all persons within the jurisdiction of the United States to the full and equal enjoyment of the accommodations, advantages, facilities, and privileges of inns, public conveyances on land or water, theaters, and other places of public amusement, and made applicable to citizens of every race and color, regardless of any previous condition of servitude, was unconstitutional and void upon the ground that the 14th Amendment was prohibitory upon the states only, and the legislation authorized to be adopted by Congress for enforcing it was not direct legislation on matters respecting which the states were prohibited from making or enforcing certain laws or doing certain acts, but was corrective legislation such as might be necessary or proper for counteracting and redressing the effect of such laws or acts. In delivering the opinion of the court Justice Bradley observed that the 14th Amendment "does not invest Congress with power to legislate upon subjects that are within the domain of state legislation; but to provide modes of relief against state legislation or state action, of the kind referred to. It does not authorize Congress to create a code of municipal law for the regulation of private rights; but to provide modes of redress against the operation of state laws, and the action of state officers, executive or judicial, when these are subversive of the fundamental rights specified in the amendment. Positive rights and privileges are undoubtedly secured by the 14th Amendment; but they are secured by way of prohibition against state laws and state proceedings affecting those rights and privileges, and by power given to Congress to legislate for the purpose of carrying such prohibition into effect; and such legislation must necessarily be predicated upon such supposed state laws or state proceedings, and be directed to the correction of their operation and effect."

. . . . While we think the enforced separation of the races, as applied to the internal commerce of the state, neither abridges the privileges or immunities of the colored man, deprives him of his property without due process of law, nor denies him the equal protection of the laws, within the meaning of the 14th Amendment, we are not prepared to say that the conductor, in assigning passengers to the coaches according to their race, does not act at this peril, or that the provision of the 2d section of the act that denies to the passenger compensation in damages for a refusal to receive him into the coach in which he properly belongs, is a valid exercise of the legislative power. Indeed, we understand it to be conceded by the state's attorney that such part of the act that exempts from liability the railway company and its officers is unconstitutional. The power to assign to a particular coach obviously implies the power to determine to which race the passenger belongs, as well as the power to determine who, under the laws of the particular state, is to be deemed a white and who a colored person. . . . [T]he only issue made [in this case] is as to the unconstitutionality of the act, so far as it requires the railway to provide separate accommodations, and the conductor to assign passengers according to their race.

It is claimed by [Plessy] that, in any mixed community, the reputation of belonging to the dominant race, in this instance the white race, is property, in the same sense that a right of action, or of inheritance, is *property*. Conceding this to be so, for the purposes of this case, we are unable to see how this statute deprives him of, or in any way

affects his right to, such property. If he be a white man
and assigned to a colored coach, he may have his action
for damages against the company for being deprived of
his so-called property. Upon the other hand, if he be a
colored man and be so assigned, he has been deprived of
no property, since he is not lawfully entitled to the reputation of being a white man.

In this connection it is also suggested that the same argument that will justify the state legislature in requiring
railways to provide separate accommodations for the two
races will also authorize them to require separate cars to
be provided for people whose hair is of a certain color, or
who are aliens, or who belong to certain nationalities, or
to enact laws requiring colored people to walk upon one
side of the street, and white people upon the other, or requiring white men's houses to be painted white, and colored men's black, or their vehicles or business signs to be
of different colors, upon the theory that one side of the
street is as good as the other, or that a house or vehicle of
one color is as good as one of another color. The reply to
all this is that every exercise of the police power must be
reasonable, and extend only to such laws as are enacted in
good faith for the promotion of the public good, and not
for the annoyance or oppression of a particular class.
Thus in *Yick Wo v. Hopkins*, it was held by this court
that a municipal ordinance of the city of San Francisco to
regulate the carrying on of public laundries within the
limits of the municipality violated the provisions of the
Constitution of the United States if it conferred upon the
municipal authorities arbitrary power, at their own will,
and without regard to discretion, in the legal sense of the
term, to give or withhold consent as to persons or places,
without regard to the competency of the persons applying,
or the propriety of the places selected for the carrying on

of the business. It was held to be a covert attempt on the part of the municipality to make an arbitrary and unjust discrimination against the Chinese race. While this was the case of a municipal ordinance a like principle has been held to apply to acts of a state legislature passed in the exercise of the police power.

So far, then, as a conflict with the 14th Amendment is concerned, the case reduces itself to the question whether the statute of Louisiana is a reasonable regulation, and with respect to this there must necessarily be a large discretion on the part of the legislature. In determining the question of reasonableness it is at liberty to act with reference to the established usages, customs, and traditions of the people, and with a view to the promotion of their comfort, and the preservation of the public peace and good order. Gauged by this standard, we cannot say that a law which authorizes or even requires the separation of the two races in public conveyances is unreasonable or more obnoxious to the 14th Amendment than the acts of Congress requiring separate schools for colored children in the District of Columbia, the constitutionality of which does not seem to have been questioned, or the corresponding acts of state legislatures.

We consider the underlying fallacy of [Plessy's] argument to consist in the assumption that the enforced separation of the two races stamps the colored race with a badge of inferiority. If this be so, it is not by reason of anything found in the act, but solely because the colored race chooses to put that construction upon it. The argument necessarily assumes that if, as has been more than once the case, and is not unlikely to be so again, the colored race should become the dominant power in the state legislature, and should enact a law in precisely similar terms, it would thereby relegate the white race to an inferior position. We imagine that the white race, at least, would not acquiesce in this assumption. The argument also assumes that social prejudices may be overcome by legislation, and that equal rights cannot be secured to the negro except by an enforced commingling of the two races. We cannot accept this proposition. If the two races are to meet on terms of social equality, it must be the result of natural affinities, a mutual appreciation of each other's merits and a voluntary consent of individuals. As was said by the court of appeals of New York in *People v. Gallagher*, "this end can neither be accomplished nor promoted by laws which conflict with the general sentiment of the community upon whom they are designed to operate. When the government, therefore, has secured to each of its citizens equal rights before the law and equal opportunities for improvement and progress, it has accomplished the end for which it is organized and performed all of the functions respecting social advantages with which it is endowed." Legislation is powerless to eradicate racial instincts or to abolish distinctions based upon physical differences, and the attempt to do so can only result in accentuating the difficulties of the present situation. If the civil and political rights of both races be equal, one cannot be inferior to the other civilly or politically. If one race be inferior to the other socially, the Constitution of the United States cannot put them upon the same plane.

It is true that the question of the proportion of colored blood necessary to constitute a colored person, as distinguished from a white person, is one upon which there is a difference of opinion in the different states, some holding that any visible admixture of black blood stamps the person as belonging to the colored race;others that it depends upon the preponderance of blood; and still others that the

predominance of white blood must only be in the proportion of three fourths. But these are questions to be determined under the laws of each state and are not properly
put in issue in this case. Under the allegation of his petition it may undoubtedly become a question of importance
whether, under the laws of Louisiana, the petitioner belongs to the white or colored race.

The judgment of the court [below] is therefore affirmed.

Plessy v. Ferguson, *which severely limited the Fourteenth
Amendment's Equal Protection Clause, was decided by an
8-1 majority. The minority of one was Justice John Marshall Harlan, who wrote in angry dissent:* "... *in the eyes
of the law, there is in this country no superior, dominant
ruling class of citizens. There is no caste here. Our Constitution is color blind and neither knows nor tolerates
classes among its citizens.*" *The racial segregation doctrine of "Separate But Equal" established in 1896 by*
Plessy *was not overruled by the United States Supreme
Court until 1954 in* Brown v. Board of Education. *(See*
Volume II *of* Civil Rights Decisions.*)*

THE CHINESE AMERICAN CASES
Yick Wo v. Hopkins

It shall be unlawful, from and after the passage of this order, for any person or persons to establish, maintain, or carry on a laundry within the corporate limits of San Francisco without first obtaining the consent of the board of supervisors, except the same be located in a building constructed either of brick or stone.

The San Francisco "Chinese Laundry" Laws

In 1880 there were about 320 laundries in San Francisco, of which about 240 were owned and operated by Chinese proprietors. Of the 320 about 310 were constructed of wood, as were nine-tenths of the houses in San Francisco. On May 26 and July 28, 1880 San Francisco's supervisors passed the "Chinese Laundry" Laws, municipal ordinances enacted obstensibly to protect the largely wooden city from fire, but whose true motive was to drive San Francisco's Chinese laundries out of business.

Yick Wo had operated a laundry in the same wooden building for twenty-two years. On July 1, 1885 he was refused consent to continue his trade. The City of San Francisco refused similar consent to over two hundred other Chinese laundrymen, while they gave their consent to eighty non-Chinese. Yick Wo and more than one hundred fifty other Chinese laundrymen were arrested, tried, and found guilty of violating the San Francisco "Chinese Laundry" Laws. Yick Wo was fined $10, which he refused to pay, and was imprisoned in the San Francisco County Jail. He petitioned the California Supreme Court to order San Francisco Sheriff Hopkins to release him. That court refused and Yick Wo, asserting that the arbitrary application of a law based solely on race was unconstitutional, appealed to the U.S. Supreme Court.

On May 10, 1886 Justice Stanley Matthews announced the 9-0 decision of the Court. The edited text follows.

THE YICK WO COURT

Chief Justice Morrison Waite
Appointed by President Grant
Served 1874 - 1888

Associate Justice Samuel Miller
Appointed by President Lincoln
Served 1862 - 1890

Associate Justice Stephen Field
Appointed by President Lincoln
Served 1863 - 1897

Associate Justice Joseph Bradley
Appointed by President Grant
Served 1870 - 1892

Associate Justice John Marshall Harlan
Appointed by President Hayes
Served 1877 - 1911

Associate Justice William Woods
Appointed by President Hayes
Served 1880 - 1887

Associate Justice Stanley Matthews
Appointed by President Garfield
Served 1881 - 1889

Associate Justice Horace Gray
Appointed by President Arthur
Served 1881 - 1902

Associate Justice Samuel Blatchford
Appointed by President Arthur
Served 1882 - 1893

The unedited text of *Yick Wo v. Hopkins* can be found on page 356, volume 118 of *United States Reports*.

YICK WO v. HOPKINS
May 10, 1886

JUSTICE MATTHEWS: In the case of the petitioner [Yick Wo], brought here [from] the Supreme Court of California, our jurisdiction is limited to the question, whether [Yick Wo] has been denied a right in violation of the Constitution, laws, or treaties of the United States. . . .

[T]his court [is not precluded] from putting upon the ordinances of the supervisors of the county and city of San Francisco an independent construction; for the determination of the question whether the proceedings under these ordinances and in enforcement of them [regulating the kind of buildings in which laundries may be located] are in conflict with the Constitution and laws of the United States, necessarily involves the meaning of the ordinances, which, for that purpose, we are required to ascertain and adjudge.

. . . . The rights of [Yick Wo], as affected by the proceedings of which [he] complain[s], are not less, because [he is an alien and subject] of the Emperor of China. By the third article of the treaty between this Government and that of China, concluded November 17, 1880, it is stipulated: "If Chinese laborers, or Chinese of any other class, now either permanently or temporarily residing in the territory of the United States, meet with ill treatment at the hands of any other persons, the Government of the United States will exert all its powers to devise measures for their protection, and to secure to them the same rights, privileges, immunities and exemptions as may be enjoyed by the citizens or subjects of the most favored nation, and to which they are entitled by treaty."

The Fourteenth Amendment to the Constitution is not confined to the protection of citizens. It says: "Nor shall any State deprive any person of life, liberty, or property without due process of law; nor deny to any person within its jurisdiction the equal protection of the laws." These provisions are universal in their application, to all persons within the territorial jurisdiction, without regard to any differences of race, of color, or of nationality; and the equal protection of the laws is a pledge of the protection of equal laws. It is accordingly enacted by Section 1977 of the Revised Statutes, that "all persons within the jurisdiction of the United States shall have the same right in every State and Territory to make and enforce contracts, to sue, be parties, give evidence, and to the full and equal benefit of all laws and proceedings for the security of persons and property as is enjoyed by white citizens and shall be subject to like punishment, pains, penalties, taxes, licenses, and exactions of every kind, and to no other." The questions we have to consider and decide in [this case], therefore, are to be treated as involving the rights of every citizen of the United States equally with those of the strangers and aliens who now invoke the jurisdiction of the court.

It is contended on the part of [Yick Wo] that the ordinances for violations of which [he is] sentenced to imprisonment, are void on their face, as being within the prohibitions of the Fourteenth Amendment; and, in the alternative, if not so, that they are void by reason of their administration, operating unequally, so as to punish in the present [petitioner] what is permitted to others as lawful, without any distinction of circumstances - an unjust and illegal discrimination, it is claimed, which, though not made expressly by the ordinances is made possible by them.

When we consider the nature and the theory of our institutions of government, the principles upon which they are supposed to rest, and review the history of their development, we are constrained to conclude that they do not mean to leave room for the play and action of purely personal and arbitrary power. Sovereignty itself is, of course, not subject to law, for it is the author and source of law; but in our system while sovereign powers are delegated to the agencies of government, sovereignty itself remains with the people, by whom and for whom all government exists and acts. And the law is the definition and limitation of power. It is, indeed, quite true, that there must always be lodged somewhere, and in some person or body, the authority of final decision; and in many cases of mere administration the responsibility is purely political, no appeal lying except to the ultimate tribunal of the public judgment, exercised either in the pressure of opinion or by means of the suffrage. But the fundamental rights to life, liberty, and the pursuit of happiness, considered as individual possessions, are secured by those maxims of constitutional law which are the monuments showing the victorious progress of the race in securing to men the blessings of civilization under the reign of just and equal laws, so that, in the famous language of the Massachusetts Bill of Rights, the government of the commonwealth "may be a government of laws and not of men." For, the very idea that one man may be compelled to hold his life, or the means of living, or any material right essential to the enjoyment of life, at the mere will of another, seems to be intolerable in any country where freedom prevails, as being the essence of slavery itself.

There are many illustrations that might be given of this truth, which would make manifest that it was self-evident in the light of our system of jurisprudence. The case of the political franchise of voting is one. Though not regarded strictly as a natural right, but as privilege merely conceded by society according to its will, under certain conditions, nevertheless it is regarded as a fundamental political right, because preservative of all rights.

. . . . In the present [case] we are not obliged to reason from the probable to the actual, and pass upon the validity of the ordinances complained of, as tried merely by the opportunities which their terms afford, of unequal and unjust discrimination in their administration. For the [case presents] the ordinances in actual operation, and the facts shown establish an administration directed so exclusively against a particular class of persons as to warrant and require the conclusion, that, whatever may have been the intent of the ordinances as adopted, they are applied by the public authorities charged with their administration, and thus representing the State itself, with a mind so unequal and oppressive as to amount to a practical denial by the State of that equal protection of the laws which is secured to [Yick Wo], as to all other persons, by the broad and benign provisions of the Fourteenth Amendment to the Constitution of the United States. Though the law itself be fair on its face and impartial in appearance, yet, if it is applied and administered by public authority with an evil eye and an unequal hand, so as practically to make unjust and illegal discriminations between persons in similar circumstances, material to their rights, the denial of equal justice is still within the prohibition of the Constitution. . . .

The present [case] . . . [is] within this class. It appears that [Yick Wo has] complied with every requisite, deemed by the law or by the public officers charged with its administration, necessary for the protection of neighboring property from fire, or as a precaution against injury to the public health. No reason whatever, except the will of the supervisors, is assigned why [he] should not be permitted to carry on, in the accustomed manner, [his] harmless and useful occupation, on which [he depends] for a livelihood. And while this consent of the supervisors is withheld from [him] and from two hundred others who have also petitioned, all of whom happen to be Chinese subjects, eighty others, not Chinese subjects, are permitted to carry on the same business under similar conditions. The fact of this discrimination is admitted. No reason for it is shown, and the conclusion cannot be resisted, that no reason for it exists except hostility to the race and nationality to which [Yick Wo belongs], and which in the eye of the law is not justified. The discrimination is, therefore, illegal, and the public administration which enforces it is a denial of the equal protection of the laws and a violation of the Fourteenth Amendment of the Constitution. The imprisonment of [Yick Wo] is, therefore, illegal, and [he] must be discharged. To this end, the judgment of the Supreme Court of California in the case of Yick Wo . . . [is reversed], and the [case] remanded [returned to the lower court], . . . with directions to discharge [Yick Wo] from custody and imprisonment.

The Yick Wo *decision, striking down San Francisco's racially drawn Chinese Laundry Laws, was one of the few successful civil rights challenges under the Fourteenth Amendment's Equal Protection Clause. Not until 1954 in* Brown v. Board of Education *did the United States Supreme Court finally strike down all legal racial segregation. (See* Volume II *of* Civil Rights Decisions.*)*

THE CHINESE AMERICAN CASES
Chae Chan Ping v. United States

From and after the passage of this act, it shall be unlawful for any Chinese laborer who shall at any time heretofore have been, or who may now or hereafter be, a resident within the United States, and who shall have departed, or shall depart therefrom, and shall not have returned, before the passage of this act, to return to, or remain in, the United States.

**The Chinese Exclusion Act
October 1, 1888**

The discovery, in 1848, of gold in California began a mass immigration of Chinese workers to the United States. By 1867 an estimated 50,000 Chinese lived and worked in California alone. Resentment of the Chinese workers led to anti-Chinese riots in Seattle in 1855 and in Los Angeles in 1871. In February 1879 the California Constitutional Convention, characterizing Chinese immigration as an "Oriental invasion" and a "menace to our civilization," asked the Congress to prevent further immigration. In reaction, the Congress passed the Chinese Exclusion Act.

On October 8, 1888, one week after the passage of the Chinese Exclusion Act, the steamship Belgic arrived in San Francisco from Hong Kong. One of the passengers, Chae Chan Ping, a Chinese worker who had lived in San Francisco since 1875, was returning home from a four month visit to his native China. At San Francisco, Ping was refused readmission to the United States based on the provisions of the Chinese Exclusion Act. Ping fought his exclusion as a violation of existing treaties between the United States and China. A Federal Court upheld Ping's exclusion and ordered him deported. Ping appealed to the United States Supreme Court.

On May 13, 1889 Justice Stephen Field announced the 8-0 decision of the Court. The edited text follows.

THE PING COURT

Chief Justice Melville Fuller
Appointed by President Cleveland
Served 1888 - 1910

Associate Justice Samuel Miller
Appointed by President Lincoln
Served 1862 - 1890

Associate Justice Stephen Field
Appointed by President Lincoln
Served 1863 - 1897

Associate Justice Joseph Bradley
Appointed by President Grant
Served 1870 - 1892

Associate Justice John Marshall Harlan
Appointed by President Hayes
Served 1877 - 1911

Associate Justice Stanley Matthews
Appointed by President Garfield
Served 1881 - 1889

Associate Justice Horace Gray
Appointed by President Arthur
Served 1881 - 1902

Associate Justice Samuel Blatchford
Appointed by President Arthur
Served 1882 - 1893

Associate Justice Lucius Lamar
Appointed by President Cleveland
Served 1888 - 1893

The unedited text of *Ping v. United States* can be found on page 581, volume 130 of *United States Reports*.

CHAE CHAN PING v. UNITED STATES
May 13, 1889

JUSTICE FIELD: The appeal involves a consideration of the validity of the act of Congress of October 1, 1888, prohibiting Chinese laborers from entering the United States who had departed before its passage, having a certificate issued under the act of 1882 as amended by the act of 1884, granting them permission to return. The validity of the act is assailed as being in effect an expulsion from the country of Chinese laborers, in violation of existing treaties between the United States and the government of China, and of rights vested in them under the laws of Congress.

. . . . The first treaty between the United States and the Empire of China was concluded [in 1844, the second in] June, 1858. . . . It reiterated the pledges of peace and friendship between the two nations, renewed the promise of protection to all citizens of the United States in China peaceably attending to their affairs, and stipulated for security to Christians in the profession of their religion. Neither the treaty of 1844, nor that of 1858, touched upon the migration and emigration of the citizens and subjects of the two nations respectively from one country to the other. . . .

It was not until the additional articles of 1868 were adopted that any public declaration was made by the two nations that there were advantages in the free migration and emigration of their citizens and subjects respectively from one country to the other; and stipulations given that each should enjoy in the country of the other, with respect to travel or residence, the "privileges, immunities, and exemptions" enjoyed by citizens or subjects of the

most favored nation. Whatever modifications have since
been made to these general provisions have been caused
by a well-founded apprehension - from the experience of
years - that a limitation to the immigration of certain
classes from China was essential to the peace of the community on the Pacific Coast, and possibly to the preservation of our civilization there. A few words on this point
may not be deemed inappropriate here, they being confined to matters of public notoriety, which have frequently been brought to the attention of Congress.

The discovery of gold in California in 1848, as is well
known, was followed by a large immigration thither from
all parts of the world, attracted not only by the hope of
gain from the mines, but from the great prices paid for all
kinds of labor. The news of the discovery penetrated
China, and laborers came from there in great numbers, a
few with their own means, but by far the greater number
under contract with employers, for whose benefit they
worked. These laborers readily secured employment, and,
as domestic servants, and in various kinds of out-door
work, proved to be exceedingly useful. For some years
little opposition. was made to them except when they
sought to work in the mines, but, as their numbers increased, they began to engage in various mechanical pursuits and trades, and thus came in competition with our
artisans and mechanics, as well as our laborers in the field.

The competition steadily increased as the laborers came in
crowds on each steamer that arrived from China, or Hong
Kong, an adjacent English port. They were generally in-
dustrious and frugal. Not being accompanied by families,
except in rare instances, their expenses were small; and
they were content with the simplest fare, such as would
not suffice for our laborers and artisans. The competition

between them and our people was for this reason altogether in their favor, and the consequent irritation, proportionately deep and bitter, was followed, in many cases, by open conflicts, to the great disturbance of the public peace.

The differences of race added greatly to the difficulties of the situation. . . . [T]hey remained strangers in the land, residing apart by themselves, and adhering to the customs and usages of their own country. It seemed impossible for them to assimilate with our people or to make any change in their habits or modes of living. As they grew in numbers each year the people of the coast saw, or believed they saw, in the facility of immigration, and in the crowded millions of China, where population presses upon the means of subsistence, great danger that at no distant day that portion of our country would be overrun by them unless prompt action was taken to restrict their immigration. The people there accordingly petitioned earnestly for protective legislation.

In December, 1878, the convention which framed the present constitution of California, being in session, took this subject up, and memorialized Congress upon it, setting forth, in substance, that the presence of Chinese laborers had a baneful effect upon the material interests of the State, and upon public morals; that their immigration was in numbers approaching the character of an Oriental invasion, and was menace to our civilization; that the discontent from this cause was not confined to any political party, or to any class or nationality, but was well-nigh universal; that they retained the habits and customs of their own country, and in fact constituted a Chinese settlement within the State, without any interest in our country or its institutions; and praying Congress to take measures to prevent their further immigration. This memorial was presented to Congress in February, 1879.

So urgent and constant were the prayers for relief against existing and anticipated evils, both from the public authorities of the Pacific Coast and from private individuals, that Congress was impelled to act on the subject. Many persons, however, both in and out of Congress, were of opinion that so long as the treaty remained unmodified, legislation restricting immigration would be a breach of faith with China. A statute was accordingly passed appropriating money to send commissioners to China to act with our minister there in negotiating and concluding by treaty a settlement of such matters of interest between the two governments as might be confided to them. Such commissioners were appointed, and as the result of their negotiations the supplementary treaty of November 17, 1880 was concluded. . . .

The government of China . . . agreed that notwithstanding the stipulation of former treaties, the United States might regulate, limit, or suspend the coming of Chinese laborers, or their residence therein, without absolutely forbidding it, whenever in their opinion the interests of the country, or of any part of it, might require such action. Legislation for such regulation, limitation, or suspension was entrusted to the discretion of our government, with the condition that it should only be such as might be necessary for that purpose, and that the immigrants should not be maltreated or abused. On the 6th of May, 1882, an act of Congress was approved, to carry this supplementary treaty into effect. It is entitled "An act to execute certain treaty stipulations relating to Chinese." Its first section declares that after ninety days from the passage of the act, and for the period of ten years from its date, the coming of Chi-

nese laborers to the United States is suspended, and that it
shall be unlawful for any such laborer to come, or, having
come, to remain within the United States. The second
makes it a misdemeanor, punishable by fine, to which imprisonment may be added, for the master of any vessel
knowingly to bring within the United States from a foreign country, and land, any such Chinese laborer. The
third provides that those two sections shall not apply to
Chinese laborers who were in the United States November
17, 1880, or who should come within ninety days after
the passage of the act. The fourth declares that, for the
purpose of identifying the laborers who were here on the
17th of November, 1880, or who should come within the
ninety days mentioned, and [a certificate would be issued]
to furnish them with "the proper evidence" of their right
to go from and come to the United States. . . .

The enforcement of this act with respect to laborers who
were in the United States on November 17, 1880, was attended with great embarrassment, from the suspicious nature, in many instances, of the testimony offered to establish the residence of the parties, arising from the loose notions entertained by the witnesses of the obligation of an
oath. This fact led to a desire for further legislation restricting the evidence receivable, and the amendatory act
of July 5, 1884, was accordingly passed. . . . To obviate
the difficulties attending its enforcement the amendatory
act of 1884 declared that the certificate which the laborer
must obtain "shall be the only evidence permissible to establish his right of re-entry" into the United States.

. . . . The same difficulties and embarrassments continued
with respect to the proof of their former residence. Parties were able to pass successfully the required examination as to their residence before November 17, 1880, who,

it was generally believed, had never visited our shores. To
prevent the possibility of the policy of excluding Chinese
laborers being evaded, the act of October 1, 1888, the validity of which is the subject of consideration in this case,
was passed. It is entitled "An act a supplement to an act
entitled 'An act to execute certain treaty stipulations relating to Chinese,' approved the sixth day of May, eighteen hundred and eighty-two." It is as follows:

"*Be it enacted by the Senate and House of Representatives of the United States of America in
Congress assembled,* That from and after the passage of this act, it shall be unlawful for any Chinese laborer who shall at any time heretofore
have been, or who may now or hereafter be, a
resident within the United States, and who shall
have departed, or shall depart therefrom, and
shall not have returned before the passage of this
act, to return to, or remain in, the United States.

"Sec. 2. That no certificates of identity provided
for in the fourth and fifth sections of the act to
which this is a supplement shall hereafter be issued; and every certificate heretofore issued in
pursuance thereof is hereby declared void and of
no effect, and the Chinese laborer claiming admission by virtue thereof shall not be permitted
to enter the United States.

"Sec. 3. That all the duties prescribed, liabilities,
penalties, and forfeitures imposed, and the powers conferred by the second, tenth, eleventh and
twelfth sections of the act to which this is a supplement, are hereby extended and made applicable to the provisions of this act.

"Sec. 4. That all such part or parts of the act to which this is a supplement as are inconsistent herewith are hereby repealed.

"Approved October 1, 1888."

The validity of this act, as already mentioned, is assailed, as being in effect an expulsion from the country of Chinese laborers in violation of existing treaties between the United States and the government of China, and of rights vested in them under the laws of Congress. The objection that the act is in conflict with the treaties was earnestly pressed in the court below, and the answer to it constitutes the principal part of its opinion. Here the objection made is, that the act of 1888 impairs a right vested under the treaty of 1880, as a law of the United States, and the statutes of 1882 and of 1884 passed in execution of it. It must be conceded that the act of 1888 is in contravention of express stipulations of the treaty of 1868 and of the supplemental treaty of 1880, but it is not on that account invalid or to be restricted in its enforcement. The treaties were of no greater legal obligation than the act of Congress. By the Constitution, laws made in pursuance thereof and treaties made under the authority of the United States are both declared to be the supreme law of the land, and no paramount authority is given to one over the other. A treaty, it is true, is in its nature a contract between nations and is often merely promissory in its character, requiring legislation to carry its stipulations into effect. Such legislation will be open to future repeal or amendment. If the treaty operates by its own force, and relates to a subject within the power of Congress, it can be deemed in that particular only the equivalent of a legislative act, to be repealed or modified at the pleasure of

Congress. In either case the last expression of the sovereign will must control.

. . . . There being nothing in the treaties between China and the United States to impair the validity of the act of Congress of October 1, 1888, was it on any other ground beyond the competency of Congress to pass it? If so, it must be because it was not within the power of Congress to prohibit Chinese laborers who had at the time departed from the United States, or should subsequently depart, from returning to the United States. Those laborers are not citizens of the United States; they are aliens. That the government of the United States, through the action of the legislative department, can exclude aliens from its territory is a proposition which we do not think open to controversy. Jurisdiction over its own territory to that extent is an incident of every independent nation. It is a part of its independence. If it could not exclude aliens it would be to that extent subject to the control of another power. As said by this court in the case of *The Exchange*, speaking by Chief Justice Marshall: "The jurisdiction of the nation within its own territory is necessarily exclusive and absolute. It is susceptible of no limitation not imposed by itself. Any restriction upon it, deriving validity from an external source, would imply a diminution of its sovereignty to the extent of the restriction, and an investment of that sovereignty to the same extent in that power which could impose such restriction. All exceptions, therefore, to the full and complete power of a nation within its own territories, must be traced up to the consent of the nation itself. They can flow from no other legitimate source."

. . . . To preserve its independence, and give security against foreign aggression and encroachment, is the highest duty of every nation, and to attain these ends nearly all other considerations are to be subordinated. It matters not in what form such aggression and encroachment come, whether from the foreign nation acting in its national character or from vast hordes of its people crowding in upon us. The government, possessing the powers which are to be exercised for protection and security, is clothed with authority to determine the occasion on which the powers shall be called forth; and its determination, so far as the subjects affected are concerned, are necessarily conclusive upon all its departments and officers. If, therefore, the government of the United States, through its legislative department, considers the presence of foreigners of a different race in this country, who will not assimilate with us, to be dangerous to its peace and security, their exclusion is not to be stayed [stopped] because at the time there are no actual hostilities with the nation of which the foreigners are subjects. The existence of war would render the necessity of the proceeding only more obvious and pressing. The same necessity, in a less pressing degree, may arise when war does not exist, and the same authority which adjudges the necessity in one case must also determine it in the other. In both cases its determination is conclusive upon the judiciary. If the government of the country of which the foreigners excluded are subjects is dissatisfied with this action it can make complaint to the executive head of our government, or resort to any other measure which, in its judgment, its interests or dignity may demand; and there lies its only remedy.

. . . . The power of exclusion of foreigners being an incident of sovereignty belonging to the government of the United States, as a part of those sovereign powers delegated by the Constitution, the right to its exercise at any time when, in the judgment of the government, the interests of the country require it, cannot be granted away or restrained on behalf of any one. The powers of government are delegated in trust to the United States, and are incapable of transfer to any other parties. They cannot be abandoned or surrendered. Nor can their exercise be hampered, when needed for the public good, by any considerations of private, interest. The exercise of these public trusts is not the subject of barter or contract. Whatever license, therefore, Chinese laborers may have obtained, previous to the act of October 1, 1888, to return to the United States after their departure, is held at the will of the government, revocable at any time, at its pleasure. Whether a proper consideration by our government of its previous laws, or a proper respect for the nation whose subjects are affected by its action, ought to have qualified its inhibition and made it applicable only to persons departing from the country after the passage of the act, are not questions for judicial determination. If there be any just ground of complaint on the part of China, it must be made to the political department of our government, which is alone competent to act upon the subject. . . .

Order affirmed [upheld].

The Chinese Exclusion Act, which denied Chae Chan Ping reentry to the United States in 1889, was broadened in 1924 by the passage of the Asian Immigration Act, which effectively excluded all Asians. These acts were repealed by the United States Congress in 1943.

THE U.S. CONSTITUTION

PREAMBLE

We the people of the United States, in order to form a more perfect union, establish justice, insure domestic tranquility, provide for the common defense, promote the general welfare, and secure the blessings of liberty to ourselves and our posterity, do ordain and establish this Constitution for the United States of America.

ARTICLE I

Section 1. All legislative powers herein granted shall be vested in a Congress of the United States, which shall consist of a Senate and House of Representatives.

Section 2. (1) The House of Representatives shall be composed of members chosen every second year by the people of several states, and the electors in each state shall have the qualifications requisite for electors of the most numerous branch of the State Legislature.

(2) No person shall be a Representative who shall not have attained to the age of twenty-five years, and been seven years a citizen of the United States, and who shall not, when elected, be an inhabitant of that state in which he shall be chosen.

(3) Representatives and direct taxes shall be apportioned among the several states which may be included within this union, according to their respective numbers, which shall be determined by adding to the whole number of free persons, including those bound to service for a term of years, and excluding Indians not taxed, three-fifths of all other persons. The actual enumeration shall be made

within three years after the first meeting of the Congress
of the United States, and within every subsequent term of
ten years, in such manner as they shall be law direct. The
number of Representatives shall not exceed one for every
thirty thousand, but each state shall have at least one Representative; and until such enumeration shall be made, the
State of New Hampshire shall be entitled to choose three,
Massachusetts eight, Rhode Island and Providence Plantations one, Connecticut five, New York six, New Jersey
four, Pennsylvania eight, Delaware one, Maryland six, Virginia ten, North Carolina five, South Carolina five, and
Georgia three.

(4) When vacancies happen in the representation from
any state, the executive authority thereof shall issue Writs
of Election to fill such vacancies.

(5) The House of Representatives shall choose their
Speaker and other Officers; and shall have the sole power
of impeachment.

Section 3. (1) The Senate of the United States shall be
composed of two Senators from each state, chosen by the
legislature thereof, for six years; and each Senator shall
have one vote.

(2) Immediately after they shall be assembled in consequence of the first election, they shall be divided as equally as may be into three classes. The seats of the Senators
of the first class shall be vacated at the expiration of the
second year, of the second class at the expiration of the
fourth year, and of the third class at the expiration of the
sixth year, so that one-third may be chosen every second
year; and if vacancies happen by resignation, or otherwise,
during the recess of the legislature of any state, the execu-

tive thereof may take temporary appointments until the next meeting of the legislature, which shall then fill such vacancies.

(3) No person shall be a Senator who shall not have attained to the age of thirty years, and been nine years a citizen of the United States, and who shall not, when elected, be an inhabitant of that state for which he shall be chosen.

(4) The Vice President of the United States shall be President of the Senate, but shall have no vote, unless they be equally divided.

(5) The Senate shall choose their other Officers, and also a President pro tempore, in the absence of the Vice President, or when he shall exercise the Office of President of the United States.

(6) The Senate shall have the sole power to try all impeachments. When sitting for that purpose, they shall be on oath or affirmation. When the President of the United States is tried, the Chief Justice shall preside: and no person shall be convicted without the concurrence of two-thirds of the members present.

(7) Judgment in cases of impeachment shall not extend further than to removal from office, and disqualification to hold and enjoy any office of honor, trust, or profit under the United States: but the party convicted shall nevertheless be liable and subject to indictment, trial, judgment, and punishment, according to law.

Section 4. (1) The times, places and manner of holding elections for Senators and Representatives, shall be pre-

scribed in each state by the legislature thereof; but the
Congress may at any time by law make or alter such regulations, except as to the places of choosing Senators.

(2) The Congress shall assemble at least once in every
year, and such meeting shall be on the first Monday in
December, unless they shall by law appoint a different
day.

Section 5. (1) Each House shall be the judge of the elections, returns, and qualifications of its own members, and
a majority of each shall constitute a quorum to do business; but a smaller number may adjourn from day to day,
and may be authorized to compel the attendance of absent
members, in such manner, and under such penalties as
each House may provide.

(2) Each House may determine the rules of its proceedings, punish its members for disorderly behavior, and,
with the concurrence of two-thirds, expel a member.

(3) Each House shall keep a journal of its proceedings,
and from time to time publish the same, excepting such
parts as may in their judgment require secrecy; and the
yeas and nays of the members of either House on any
question shall, at the desire of one-fifth of those present,
be entered on the journal.

(4) Neither House, during the Session of Congress, shall,
without the consent of the other, adjourn for more than
three days, nor to any other place than that in which the
two Houses shall be sitting.

Section 6. (1) The Senators and Representatives shall receive a compensation for their services, to be ascertained

by law, and paid out of the Treasury of the United States. They shall in all cases, except treason, felony and breach of the peace, be privileged from arrest during their attendance at the session of their respective Houses, and in going to and returning from the same; and for any speech or debate in either House, they shall not be questioned in any other place.

(2) No Senator or Representative shall, during the time for which he was elected, be appointed to any civil office under the authority of the United States, which shall have been created, or the emoluments whereof shall have been increased during such time and no person holding any office under the United States, shall be a member of either House during his continuance in office.

Section 7. (1) All bills for raising revenue shall originate in the House of Representatives; but the Senate may propose or concur with amendments as on other bills.

(2) Every bill which shall have passed the House of Representatives and the Senate, shall, before it become a law, be presented to the President of the United States; if he approve he shall sign it, but if not he shall return it, with his objections to the House in which it shall have originated, who shall enter the objections at large on their journal, and proceed to reconsider it. If after such reconsideration two-thirds of that House shall agree to pass the bill, it shall be sent together with the objections, to the other House, by which it shall likewise be reconsidered, and if approved by two-thirds of that House, it shall become a law. But in all such cases the votes of both Houses shall be determined by yeas and nays, and the names of the persons voting for and against the bill shall be entered on the journal of each House respectively. If any bill shall not

be returned by the President within ten days (Sundays excepted) after it shall have been presented to him, the same shall be a law, in like manner as if he had signed it, unless the Congress by their adjournment prevent its return in which case it shall not be a law.

(3) Every order, resolution, of vote, to which the concurrence of the Senate and House of Representatives may be necessary (except on a question of adjournment) shall be presented to the President of the United States; and before the same shall take effect, shall be approved by him, or being disapproved by him, shall be repassed by two-thirds of the Senate and House of Representatives, according to the rules and limitations prescribed in the case of a bill.

Section 8. (1) The Congress shall have the power to lay and collect taxes, duties, imposts and excises, to pay the debts and provide for the common defense and general welfare of the United States; but all duties, imposts and excises shall be uniform throughout the United States;

(2) To borrow money on the credit of the United States;

(3) To regulate commerce with foreign nations, and among the several states, and with the Indian Tribes;

(4) To establish an uniform Rule of Naturalization, and uniform laws on the subject of bankruptcies throughout the United States;

(5) To coin money, regulate the value thereof, and of foreign coin, and fix the standard of weights and measures;

(6) To provide for the punishment of counterfeiting the securities and current coin of the United States;

(7) To establish Post Offices and Post Roads;

(8) To promote the progress of science and useful arts, by securing for limited times to authors and inventors the exclusive right to their respective writings and discoveries;

(9) To constitute tribunals inferior the Supreme Court;

(10) To define and punish piracies and felonies committed on the high seas,.and offenses against the Law of Nations;

(11) To declare war, grant Letters of Marque and Reprisal, and make rules concerning captures on land and water;

(12) To raise and support armies, but no appropriation of money to that use shall be for a longer term than two years;

(13) To provide and maintain a Navy;

(14) To make rules for the government and regulation of the land and naval forces;

(15) To provide for calling forth the Militia to execute the laws of the Union, suppress insurrections and repel invasions;

(16) To provide for organizing, arming, and disciplining, the Militia, and for governing such part of them as may be employed in the service of the United States, reserving to the states respectively, the appointment of the Officers,

and the authority of training the Militia according to the discipline prescribed by Congress;

(17) To exercise exclusive legislation in all cases whatsoever, over such district (not exceeding ten miles square) as may, be cession of particular states, and the acceptance of Congress, become the Seat of the Government of the United States, and to exercise like authority over all places purchased by the consent of the legislature of the state in which the same shall be, for the erection of forts, magazines, arsenals, dockyards, and other needful buildings; -- and

(18) To make all laws which shall be necessary and proper for carrying into execution the foregoing powers, and all other powers vested by this Constitution in the Government of the United States, or in any Department or Officer thereof.

Section 9. (1) The migration or importation of such persons as any of the states now existing shall think proper to admit, shall not be prohibited by the Congress prior to the year one thousand eight hundred and eight, but a tax or duty may be imposed on such importation, not exceeding ten dollars for each person.

(2) The privilege of the Writ of Habeas Corpus shall not be suspended, unless when in cases of rebellion or invasion the public safety may require it.

(3) No Bill of Attainder or ex post facto law shall be passed.

(4) No capitation, or other direct, tax shall be laid, unless in proportion to the Census or enumeration herein before directed to be taken.

(5) No tax or duty shall be laid on articles exported from any state.

(6) No preference shall be given by any regulation of commerce or revenue to th ports of one state over those of another: nor shall vessels bound to, or from, one state be obliged to enter, clear, or pay duties in another.

(7) No money shall be drawn from the Treasury, but in consequence eof `appropriations made by law; and a regular statement and account of the receipts and expenditures of all public money shall be published from time to time.

(8) No title of nobility shall be granted by the United States: and no person holding any office of profit or trust under them, shall, without the consent of the Congress, accept of any present, emolument, office, or title, of any kind whatever, from any King, Prince, or foreign State.

Section 10. (1) No state shall enter into any treaty, alliance, or confederation; grant Letter of Marque and Reprisal; coin money; emit bills of credit; make any thing but gold and silver coin a tender in payment of debts; pass and Bill of Attainder, ex post facto law, or law impairing the obligation of contracts, or grant any title of nobility.

(2) No state shall, without the consent of the Congress, lay any imposts or duties on imports or exports, except what may be absolutely necessary for executing its inspection laws: and the net produce of all duties and imposts, laid by any state on imports or exports, shall be for the use of

the Treasury of the United States; and all such laws shall be subject to the revision and control of the Congress.

(3) No state shall, without the consent of Congress, lay any duty of tonnage, keep troops, or ships of war in time of peace, enter into any agreement or compact with another state, or with a foreign power, or engage in war, unless actually invaded, or in such imminent danger as will not admit of delay.

ARTICLE II

Section 1. (1) The executive power shall be vested in a President of the United States of America. He shall hold his office during the term of four years, and, together with the Vice President, chosen for the same term, be elected, as follows:

(2) Each state shall appoint, in such manner as the legislature thereof may direct, a number of electors, equal to the whole number of Senators and Representatives to which the state may be entitled in the Congress; but no Senator or Representative, or person holding an office of trust or profit under the United States, shall be appointed an Elector.

(3) The Electors shall meet in their respective states, and vote by ballot for two persons, of whom one at least shall not be an inhabitant of the same state with themselves. And they shall make a list of all the persons voted for, and of the number of votes for each; which list they shall sign and certify, and transmit sealed to the Seat of the Government of the United States, directed to the President of the Senate. The President of the Senate shall, in the presence of the Senate and House of Representatives,

open all the certificates, and the votes shall then be counted. The person having the greatest number of votes shall be the President, if such number be a majority of the whole number of Electors appointed; and if there be more than one who have such majority, and have an equal number of votes, then the House of Representatives shall immediately choose by ballot one of them for President; and if no person have a majority, then from the five highest on the list the said House shall in like manner choose the President. But in choosing the President, the votes shall be taken by states the representation from each state having one vote; a quorum for this purpose shall consist of a member or members from two-thirds of the states, and a majority of all the states shall be necessary to a choice. In every case, after the choice of the President, the person having the greater number of votes of the Electors shall be the Vice President. But if there should remain two or more who have equal votes, the Senate shall choose from them by ballot the Vice President.

(4) The Congress may determine the time of choosing the Electors, and the day on which they shall give their votes; which day shall be the same throughout the United States.

(5) No person except a natural born citizen, or a citizen of the United States, at the time of the adoption of this Constitution, shall be eligible to the Office of President; neither shall any person be eligible to that Office who shall not have attained to the age of thirty-five years, and been fourteen years a resident within the United States.

(6) In case of the removal of the President from Office, or of his death, resignation or inability to discharge the powers and duties of the said Office, the same shall devolve on the Vice President, and the Congress may by law

provide for the case of removal, death, resignation of inability, both of the President and Vice President, declaring what Officer shall then act as President, and such Officer shall act accordingly, until the disability be removed, or a President shall be elected.

(7) The President shall, at stated times, receive for his services, a compensation, which shall neither be increased nor diminished during the period for which he shall have been elected, and he shall not receive within that period any other emolument from the United States, or any of them.

(8) Before he enter on the execution of his Office, he shall take the following Oath or Affirmation: "I do solemnly swear (or affirm) that I will faithfully execute the Office of President of the United States, and will to the best of my ability, preserve, protect and defend the Constitution of the United States."

Section 2. (1) The President shall be Commander in Chief of the Army and Navy of the United States, and of the militia of the several states, when called into the actual service of the United States; he may require the opinion, in writing, of the principal Officer in each of the Executive Departments, upon any subject relating to the duties of their respective Offices, and he shall have power to grant reprieves and pardons for offenses against the United States, except in cases of impeachment.

(2) He shall have power, by and with the advice and consent of the Senate to make treaties, provided two-thirds of the Senators present concur; and he shall nominate, and by and with the advice and consent of the Senate, shall appoint Ambassadors, other public Ministers and Consuls,

Judges of the supreme Court, and all other Officers of the United States, whose appointments are not herein otherwise provided for, and which shall be established by law; but the Congress may be law vest the appointment of such inferior Officers, as they think proper, in the President alone, in the courts of law, or in the Heads of Departments.

(3) The President shall have power to fill up all vacancies that may happen during the recess of the Senate, by granting commissions which shall expire at the end of their next Session.

Section 3. He shall from time to time give to the Congress information of the State of the Union, and recommend to their consideration such measures as he shall judge necessary and expedient; he may, on extraordinary occasions, convene both Houses, or either of them, and in case of disagreement between them, with respect to the time of adjournment, he may adjourn them to such time as he shall think proper; he shall receive Ambassadors and other public Ministers; he shall take care that the laws be faithfully executed, and shall commission all the Officers of the United States.

Section 4. The President, Vice President and all civil Officers of the United States, shall be removed from office on impeachment for, and conviction of, treason, bribery, or other high crimes and misdemeanors.

ARTICLE III

Section 1. The judicial power of the United States, shall be vested in one supreme Court, and in such inferior courts as the Congress may from time to time ordain and establish. The Judges, both of the supreme and inferior courts, shall hold their Offices during good behaviour, and shall, at stated times, receive for their services a compensation, which shall not be diminished during their continuance in office.

Section 2. (1) The judicial power shall extend to all cases, in law and equity, arising under this Constitution, the laws of the United States, and treaties made, or which shall be made, under their authority; – to all cases affecting Ambassadors, other public Ministers and Consuls; – to all cases of admiralty and maritime jurisdiction; – to controversies to which the United States shall be a party; – to controversies between two or more states; -- between a state and citizens of another state; – between citizens of different states;, – between citizens of the same state claiming lands under the grants of different states, and between a state, or the citizens thereof, and foreign states, citizens or subjects.

(2) In all cases affecting Ambassadors, other public Ministers and Consuls, and those in which a state shall be a party, the supreme Court shall have original jurisdiction. In all the other cases before mentioned, the supreme Court shall have appellate jurisdiction, both as to law and fact, with such exceptions, and under such regulations as the Congress shall make.

(3) The trial of all crimes, except in cases of impeachment, shall be by jury; and such trial shall be held in the state where the said crimes shall have been committed; but when not committed within any state, the trial shall be at such place or places as the Congress may be law have directed.

Section 3. (1) Treason against the United States, shall consist only in levying war against them, or, in adhering to their enemies, giving them aid and comfort. No person shall be convicted of treason unless on the testimony of two witnesses to the same overt act, or on confession in open Court.

(2) The Congress shall have power to declare the punishment of treason, but no Attainder of Treason shall work corruption of blood, or forfeiture except during the life of the person attainted.

ARTICLE IV

Section 1. Full faith and credit shall be given in each state to the public acts, records, and judicial proceedings of every other state. And the Congress may by general laws prescribe the manner in which such acts, records and proceedings shall be proved, and the effect thereof.

Section 2. (1) The citizens of each state shall be entitled to all privileges and immunities of citizens in the several states.

(2) A person charged in any state with treason, felony, or other crime, who shall flee from justice, and be found in another state, shall on demand of the executive authority of the state from which he fled, be delivered up, to be removed to the state having jurisdiction of the crime.

(3) No person held to service or labour in one state, under the laws thereof, escaping into another, shall, in consequence of any law or regulation therein, be discharged from such service or labour, but shall be delivered up on

claim of the party to whom such service or labour may be due.

Section 3. (1) New states may be admitted by the Congress into this Union; but no new state shall be formed or erected within the jurisdiction of any other state; nor any state be formed by the junction of two or more states, or parts of states, without the consent of the legislatures of the states concerned as well as of the Congress.

(2) The Congress shall have power to dispose of and make all needful rules and regulations respecting the territory or other property belonging to the United States; and nothing in this Constitution shall be so construed as to prejudice any claims of the United States, or of any particular state.

Section 4. The United States shall guarantee to every state in this Union a Republican form of government, and shall protect each of them against invasion; and on application of the Legislature, or of the Executive (when the Legislature cannot be convened) against domestic violence.

ARTICLE V

The Congress, whenever two-thirds of both Houses shall deem it necessary, shall propose amendments to this Constitution, or, on the application of the Legislatures of two-thirds of the several states, shall call a convention for proposing amendments, which, in either case, shall be valid to all intents and purposes, as part of this constitution, when ratified by the Legislatures of three-fourths of the several states, or by conventions in three-fourths thereof, as the one or the other mode of ratification may be proposed by the Congress; provided that no amendment which may be made prior to the year one thousand eight hundred and eight shall in any manner affect the first and fourth clauses in the Ninth Section of the first Article; and that no state, without its consent, shall be deprived of its equal suffrage in the Senate.

ARTICLE VI

(1) All debts contracted and engagements entered into, before the adoption of this Constitution shall be as valid against the United States under this Constitution, as under the Confederation.

(2) This Constitution, and the laws of the United States which shall be made in pursuance thereof; and all treaties made, or which shall be made, under the authority of the United States, shall be the supreme law of the land; and the Judges in every state shall be bound thereby, any thing in the Constitution or laws of any state to the contrary notwithstanding.

(3) The Senators and Representatives before mentioned, and the Members of the several State Legislatures, and all executive and judicial Officers, both of the United States and of the several states, shall be bound by oath or affirmation, to support this Constitution; but no religious test shall ever be required as a qualification to any Office or public trust under the United States.

ARTICLE VII

The ratification of the Conventions of nine states shall be sufficient for the establishment of this Constitution between the states so ratifying the same.

AMENDMENT I (1791)

Congress shall make no law respecting an establishment of religion, or prohibiting the free exercise thereof; or abridging the freedom of speech, or of the press; or the right of the people peaceably to assemble, and to petition the Government for a redress of grievances.

AMENDMENT II (1791)

A well regulated Militia, being necessary to the security of a free State, the right of the people to keep and bear arms, shall not be infringed.

AMENDMENT III (1791)

No soldier shall, in time of peace be quartered in any house, without the consent of the owner, nor in time of war, but in a manner to be prescribed by law.

AMENDMENT IV (1791)

The right of the people to be secure in their persons, houses, papers, and effects, against unreasonable searches and seizures, shall not be violated, and no warrants shall issue, but upon probable cause, supported by oath or affirmation, and particularly describing the place to be searched, and the persons or things to be seized.

AMENDMENT V (1791)

No person shall be held to answer for a capital, or otherwise infamous crime, unless on a presentment or indictment of a Grand Jury, except in cases arising in the land or naval forces, or in the Militia, when in actual service in time of war or public danger; nor shall any person be subject for the same offense to be twice put in jeopardy of life or limb; nor shall be compelled in any criminal case to be a witness against himself, nor be deprived of life, liberty, or property, without due process of law; nor shall private property be taken for public use, without just compensation.

AMENDMENT VI (1791)

In all criminal prosecutions, the accused shall enjoy the right to a speedy and public trial, by an impartial jury of the state and district wherein the crime shall have been committed, which district shall have been previously ascertained by law, and to be informed of the nature and cause of the accusation; to be confronted with the witnesses against him; to have compulsory process for obtaining witnesses in his favor, and to have the assistance of counsel for his defense.

AMENDMENT VII (1791)

In suits at common law, where the value in controversy shall exceed twenty dollars, the right of trial by jury shall be preserved, and no fact tried by jury, shall be otherwise re-examined in any Court of the United States, than according to the rules of the common law.

AMENDMENT VIII (1791)

Excessive bail shall not be required, nor excessive fines imposed, nor cruel and unusual punishments inflicted.

AMENDMENT IX (1791)

The enumeration in the Constitution, of certain rights, shall not be construed to deny or disparage others retained by the people.

AMENDMENT X (1791)

The powers not delegated to the United States by the Constitution, nor prohibited by it to the States, are reserved to the States respectively, or to the people.

AMENDMENT XI (1798)

The judicial power of the United States shall not be construed to extend to any suit in law or equity, commenced or prosecuted against one of the United States by citizens of another state, or by citizens or subjects of any foreign state.

AMENDMENT XII (1804)

The Electors shall meet in their respective states and vote by ballot for President and Vice-President, one of whom, at least, shall not be an inhabitant of the same stat with themselves; they shall name in their ballots the person voted for as President, and in distinct ballots the person voted for as Vice-President, and they shall make distinct lists of all persons voted for as President, and of all persons voted for as Vice-President, and of the number of votes for each, which lists they shall sign and certify, and transmit sealed to the seat of the government of the United States, directed to the President of the Senate; – the President of the Senate shall, in the presence of the Senate and House of Representatives, open all the certificates and the votes shall then be counted; — the person having the greatest number of votes for President, shall be the President, if such number be a majority of the persons having the highest numbers not exceeding three on the list of those voted for as President, the House of Representatives shall choose immediately, by ballot, the President. But in choosing the President, the votes shall be taken by states, the representation from each state having one vote; a quorum for his purpose shall consist of a member or members from two-thirds of the states, and a majority of all the states shall be necessary to a choice. And if the House of Representatives shall not choose a President whenever the right of choice shall devolve upon them before the fourth day of March next following, then the Vice-President shall act as President, as in the case of the death or other constitutional disability of the President. — The person having the greatest number of votes as Vice-President, shall be the Vice-President, if such number be a majority of the whole number of Electors appointed, and if no person have a majority, then from the two highest numbers on the list, the Senate shall choose the Vice-President; a quorum for the purpose shall consist of two-thirds of the whole number of Senators, and a majority of the whole number shall be necessary to a choice. But no person constitutionally ineligible to the office of President shall be eligible to that of Vice-President of the United States.

AMENDMENT XIII (1865)

Section 1. Neither slavery nor involuntary servitude, except as a punishment for crime whereof the party shall have been duly convicted, shall exist within the United States, or any place subject to their jurisdiction.

Section 2. Congress shall have power to enforce this article by appropriate legislation.

AMENDMENT XIV (1868)

Section 1. All persons born or naturalized in the United States, and subject to the jurisdiction thereof, are citizens of the United States and of the state wherein they reside. No state shall make or enforce any law which shall abridge the privileges or immunities of citizens of the United States; nor shall any state deprive any person of life, liberty, or property, without due process of law; nor deny to any person within its jurisdiction the equal protection of the laws.

Section 2. Representatives shall be apportioned among the several states according to their respective numbers, counting the whole number of persons in each State excluding Indians not taxed. But when the right to vote at any election for the choice of electors for President and Vice President of the United States, Representatives in Congress, the Executive and Judicial officers of a state, or the members of the Legislature thereof, is denied to any of the male inhabitants of such state, being twenty-one years of age, and citizens of the United States, or in any way abridged, except for participation in rebellion, or other crime, the basis of representation therein shall be reduced in the proportion which the number of such male citizens shall bear to the whole number of male citizens twenty-one years of age in such state.

Section 3. No person shall be a Senator or Representative in Congress, or elector of President and Vice President, or hold any office, civil or military, under the United States, or under any state, who having previously taken an oath, as a member of Congress, or as an officer of the United States, or as a member of any state legislature, or as an executive or judicial officer of any state, to support the Constitution of the United States, shall have engaged in insurrection or rebellion against the same, or given aid or comfort to the enemies thereof. But Congress may by a vote of two-thirds of each House, remove such disability.

Section 4. The validity of the public debt of the United States, authorized by law, including debts incurred for payment of pensions and bounties for services in suppressing insurrection or rebellion, shall not be questioned. But neither the United States nor any state shall assume or pay any debt or obligation incurred in aid of insurrection or rebellion against the United States, or any claim for the loss or emancipation of any slave; but all such debts, obligations and claims shall be held illegal and void.

Section 5. The Congress shall have power to enforce, by appropriate legislation, the provisions of this article.

AMENDMENT XV (1870)

Section 1. The right of citizens of the United States to vote shall not be denied or abridged by the United States or by any state on account of race, color, or previous condition of servitude.

Section 2. The Congress shall have power to enforce this article by appropriate legislation.

AMENDMENT XVI (1913)

The Congress shall have power to lay and collect taxes on income, from whatever source derived, without apportionment among the several states, and without regard to any census or enumeration.

AMENDMENT XVII (1913)

(1) The Senate of the United States shall be composed of two Senators from each state, elected by the people thereof, for six years; and each Senator shall have one vote. The electors in each State shall have the qualifications requisite for electors of the most numerous branch of the state legislatures.

(2) When vacancies happen in the representation of any state in the Senate, the executive authority of such state shall issue writs of election to fill such vacancies: *provided,* that the legislature of any state may empower the executive thereof to make temporary appointments until the people fill the vacancies by election as the legislature may direct.

(3) This amendment shall not be so construed as to affect the election or term of any Senator chosen before it becomes valid as part of the Constitution.

AMENDMENT XVIII (1919)

Section 1. After one year from the ratification of this article the manufacture, sale, or transportation of intoxicating liquors within, the importation thereof into, or the exportation thereof from the United States and all territory subject to the jurisdiction thereof for beverage purposes is hereby prohibited.

Section 2. The Congress and the several states shall have concurrent power to enforce this article by appropriate legislation.

Section 3. This article shall be inoperative unless it shall have been ratified as an amendment to the Constitution by the legislatures of the several states, as provided in the Constitution, within seven years from the date of the submission hereof to the states by the Congress.

AMENDMENT XIX (1920)

(1) The right of citizens of the United States to vote shall not be denied or abridged by the United States or by any state on account of sex.

(2) Congress shall have power to enforce this article by appropriate legislation.

AMENDMENT XX (1933)

Section 1. The terms of the President and Vice President shall end at noon on the 20th day of January, and the terms of Senators and Representatives at noon on the 3d day of January, of the years in which such terms would have ended if this article had not been ratified; and the terms of their successors shall then begin.

Section 2. The Congress shall assemble at least once in every year, and such meeting shall begin at noon on the 3d day of January, unless they shall by law appoint a different day.

Section 3. If, at the time fixed for the beginning of the term of the President, the President elect shall have died, the Vice President elect shall become President. If the President shall not have been chosen before the time fixed for the beginning of his term, or if the President elect shall have failed to qualify, then the Vice President elect shall act as President until a President shall have qualified; and the Congress may by law provide for the case wherein neither a President elect nor a Vice President elect shall have qualified, declaring who shall then act as President, or the manner in which one who is to act shall be selected, and such person shall act accordingly until a President or Vice President shall have qualified.

Section 4. The Congress may by law provide for the case of the death of any of the persons from whom the House of Representatives may choose a President whenever the right of choice shall have devolved upon them, and for the case of the death of any of the persons from whom the Senate may choose a Vice President whenever the right of choice shall have devolved upon them.

Section 5. Sections 1 and 2 shall take effect on the 15th day of October following the ratification of this article.

Section 6. This article shall be inoperative unless it shall have been ratified as an amendment to the Constitution by the legislatures of three-fourths of the several states within seven years from the date of its submission.

AMENDMENT XXI (1933)

Section 1. The eighteenth article of amendment to the Constitution of the United States is hereby repealed.

Section 2. The transportation or importation into any state, territory, or possession of the United States for delivery or use therein of intoxicating liquors, in violation of the laws thereof, is hereby prohibited.

Section 3. This article shall be inoperative unless it shall have been ratified as an amendment to the Constitution by conventions in the several states, as provided in the Constitution, within seven years from the date of the submission hereof to the states by the Congress.

AMENDMENT XXII (1951)

Section 1. No person shall be elected to the office of the President more than twice, and no person who has held the office of President, or acted as President, for more than two ears of a term to which some other person was elected President shall be elected to the office of President more than once. But this Article shall not apply to any person holding the office of President when this Article was proposed by the Congress, and shall not prevent any person who may be holding the office of President, or acting as President, during the term within which this Article becomes operative from holding the office of President or acting as President during the remainder of such term.

Section 2. This article shall be inoperative unless it shall have been ratified as an amendment to the Constitution by the legislatures of three-fourths of the several states within seven years from the date of its submission to the states by the Congress.

AMENDMENT XXIII (1961)

Section 1. The District constituting the seat of Government of the United States shall appoint in such manner as the Congress may direct:

A number of electors of President and Vice President equal to the whole number of Senators and Representatives in Congress to which the District would be entitled if it were a state, but in no event more than the least populous state; they shall be in addition to those appointed by the states, but they shall be considered, for the purposes of the election of President and Vice President, to be electors appointed by a state; and they shall meet in the District and perform such duties as provided by the twelfth article of amendment.

Section 2. The Congress shall have power to enforce this article by appropriate legislation.

AMENDMENT XXIV (1964)

Section 1. The right of citizens of the United States to vote in any primary or other election for President or Vice President, for electors for President or Vice President, or for Senator or Representative in Congress, shall not be denied or abridged by the United States, or any state by reason of failure to pay any poll tax or other tax.

Section 2. The Congress shall have power to enforce this article by appropriate legislation.

AMENDMENT XXV (1967)

Section 1. In case of the removal of the President from office or of his death or resignation, the Vice President shall become President.

Section 2. Whenever there is a vacancy in the office of the Vice President, the President shall nominate a Vice President who shall take office upon confirmation by a majority vote of both Houses of Congress.

Section 3. Whenever the President transmits to the President pro tempore of the Senate and the Speaker of the House of Representatives his written declaration that he is unable to discharge the powers and duties of his office, and until he transmits to them a written declaration to the contrary, such powers and duties shall be discharged by the Vice President as Acting President.

Section 4. Whenever the Vice President and a majority of either the principal officers of the executive departments or of such other body as Congress may by law provide, transmit to the President pro tempore of the Senate and the Speaker of the House of Representatives their written declaration that the President is unable to discharge the powers and duties of his office, the Vice President shall immediately assume the powers and duties of the office as Acting President.

Thereafter, when the President transmits to the President pro tempore of the Senate and the Speaker of the House of Representatives his written declaration that no inability exists, he shall resume the powers and duties of his office unless the Vice President and a majority of either the principal officers of the executive department or of such other body as Congress may by law provide, transmit within four days to the President pro tempore of the Senate and the Speaker of the House of Representatives their written declaration and the President is unable to discharge the powers and duties of his office. Thereupon Congress shall decide the issue, assembling within forty-eight hours for that purpose if not in session. If the Congress, within twenty-one days after receipt of the latter written declaration, or, if Congress is not in session, within twenty-one days after Congress is required to assemble, determines by two-thirds vote of both Houses that the President is unable to discharge the power and duties of his office, the Vice President shall continue to discharge the same as Acting President; otherwise, the President shall resume the powers and duties of his office.

AMENDMENT XXVI (1971)

Section 1. The right of citizens of the United States, who are eighteen years of age or older, to vote shall not be denied or abridged by the United States or by any state on account of age.

Section 2. The Congress shall have power to enforce this article by appropriate legislation.

AMENDMENT XXVII (1992)

No law, varying the compensation for the services of the Senators and Representatives, shall take effect, until an election of Representatives shall have intervened.

BIBLIOGRAPHY

THE NATIVE AMERICAN CASES

Anderson, William L., Editor, *Cherokee Removal: Before and After*, Athens, GA: University of Georgia Press, 1991.

Ehle, John, *Trail of Tears: The Rise and Fall of the Cherokee Nation*, New York, NY: Doubleday, 1988.

Filler, Louis, *The Removal of the Cherokee Nation: Manifest Destiny or National Dishonor?*, Boston, MA: Heath, 1966.

Lumpkin, Wilson, *The Removal of the Cherokee Indians from Georgia*, New York, NY: Arno Press, 1969.

Parker, Thomas V., *The Cherokee Indians, with Special Reference to their Relations With the United States Government*, New York: Grafton Press, 1907.

THE AFRICAN AMERICAN CASES

Brooke, J.T., *Short Notes on the Dred Scott Case*. Cincinnati: Moore, Wilstach, Keys & Co., 1861.

Campbell, Stanley W., *The Slave Catchers: Enforcement of the Fugitive Slave Law, 1850-1860*, Chapel Hill, NC: University of North Carolina Press, 1970.

Ehrlich, Walter, *They Have No Rights: Dred Scott's Struggle for Freedom*, New York: Greenwood Press, 1979.

Fehrenbacher, Don, *Slavery, Law & Politics: The Dred Scott Case in Historical Perspective*, New York: Oxford University Press, 1981.

Lofgren, Charles A., *The Plessy Case: A Legal-Historical Interpretation*, New York, NY: Oxford University Press, 1987.

May, Samuel, *The Fugitive Slave Law and Its Victims*, New York, NY: American Anti-Slavery Society, 1861.

Olsen, Otto H., *The Thin Disguise: Turning Point in Negro History; Plessy v. Ferguson: A Documentary Presentation, 1864-1896*, New York, NY: Humanities Press, 1967.

Stewart, James B., *Holy Warriors: The Abolitionists and American Slavery*, New York: Hill & Wang, 1976.

Wilson, Charles Morrow, *The Dred Scott Decision*, Philadelphia: Auerbach Publishers, 1973.

THE CHINESE AMERICAN CASES

Chen, Helen, *Chinese Immigration Into the United States: An analysis of Changes in Immigration Policies*, Ann Arbor, MI: University Microfilms Inc., 1980.

Sung, Betty Lee, *The Story of the Chinese in America*, New York, NY: Collier Books, 1967.

THE SUPREME COURT

Abraham, Henry Julian, *Freedom and the Court: Civil Rights and Liberties in the United States*, New York, NY: Oxford University Press, 1967.

Agresto, John, *The Supreme Court and Constitutional Democracy*, Ithaca, NY: Cornell University Press, 1984.

Braeman, John, *Before the Civil Rights Revolution: The Old Court and Individual Rights*, New York, NY: Green wood Press, 1988.

Cox, Archibald, *The Court and the Constitution*, New York, NY: Houghton-Mifflin, 1988.

Dumbauld, Edward, *The Bill of Rights and What It Means Today*, New York, NY: Greenwood Press, 1979.

Ginger, Ann Fagan, *The Law, The Supreme Court, and The People's Rights*, Woodbury, NY: Barron's Educational Series, 1973.

Goode, Stephen, *The Controversial Court: Supreme Court Influences on American Life*, New York, NY: Messner, 1982.

Kairys, David, *With Liberty and Justice for Some*, New York, NY: The New Press, 1993.

Lawson, Don, *Landmark Supreme Court Cases*, Hillside: Enslow Publishers, Inc., 1987.

Rehnquist, William H., *The Supreme Court: How It Was, How It Is,* New York, NY: Morrow, 1987.

Woodward, Bob, and Scott Armstrong, *The Brethren: Inside the Supreme Court,* New York, NY: Simon & Schuster, 1979.

Yudof, Mark, *When Government Speaks: Politics, Law, and Government Expression in America,* Berkeley, CA: University of California Press, 1983.

INDEX

EXCELLENT BOOKS ORDER FORM

(Please xerox this form so it will be available to other readers.)

Please send

Copy(ies)

_____ of CIVIL RIGHTS DECISIONS I @ $16.95 each

_____ of CIVIL RIGHTS DECISIONS II @ $16.95 each

_____ of LANDMARK DECISIONS @ $14.95 each

_____ of LANDMARK DECISIONS II @ $15.95 each

_____ of LANDMARK DECISIONS III @ $15.95 each

_____ of LANDMARK DECISIONS IV @ $15.95 each

_____ of THE ADA HANDBOOK @ $15.95 each

_____ of ABORTION DECISIONS: THE 1970's @ $15.95 each

_____ of ABORTION DECISIONS: THE 1980's @ $15.95 each

_____ of ABORTION DECISIONS: THE 1990's @ $15.95 each

_____ of JOHN F. KENNEDY: WORD FOR WORD @ $19.95 each

_____ of THOMAS JEFFERSON: WORD FOR WORD @ $19.95 each

_____ of ABRAHAM LINCOLN: WORD FOR WORD @ $19.95 each

Name: _____

Address: _____

City: _____ **State:** _____ **Zip:** _____

Add $1 per book for shipping and handling
California residents add sales tax

OUR GUARANTEE: Any Excellent Book may be returned at any time for any reason and a full refund will be made.

Mail your check or money order to: Excellent Books, Post Office Box 927105, San Diego, California 92192-7105 or call (619) 457-4895